Routledge Revivals

Foundations of Faith Volume 2

Originally published in 1925, this is the second of four volumes to discuss Christian Theology, under the guidance of the historic decisions of the Christian Church and the prevailing tendencies of Catholic thought in the early 20th Century. This volume deals with the specific beliefs connected with the person of Christ.

Foundations of Faith Volume 2
Christological

W.E. Orchard

First published in 1925 by George Allen & Unwin Ltd.

This edition first published in 2024 by Routledge
4 Park Square, Milton Park, Abingdon, Oxon, OX14 4RN

and by Routledge
605 Third Avenue, New York, NY 10158.

Routledge is an imprint of the Taylor & Francis Group, an informa business

© 1925 W.E. Orchard.

The right of W.E. Orchard to be identified as the author of this work has been asserted by him in accordance with sections 77 and 78 of the Copyright, Designs and Patents Act 1988.

All rights reserved. No part of this book may be reprinted or reproduced or utilised in any form or by any electronic, mechanical, or other means, now known or hereafter invented, including photocopying and recording, or in any information storage or retrieval system, without permission in writing from the publishers.

ISBN 13: 978-1-032-89962-6 (hbk)
ISBN 13: 978-1-003-54554-5 (ebk)
ISBN 13: 978-1-032-89964-0 (pbk)
Book DOI 10.4324/9781003545545

FOUNDATIONS OF FAITH

II
CHRISTOLOGICAL

BY THE
REV. W. E. ORCHARD, D.D.

LONDON: GEORGE ALLEN & UNWIN LTD
RUSKIN HOUSE, 40 MUSEUM STREET, W.C.1

First published in 1925

(All rights reserved)

PRINTED BY UNWIN BROTHERS, LIMITED
LONDON AND WOKING, GREAT BRITAIN

PREFACE

THIS volume is the second of a projected series of four which will endeavour to cover the whole ground of Christian Theology, under the guidance of the historic decisions of the Christian Church and the prevailing tendencies of Catholic thought, but presented in a reasonable way and with special reference to modern problems and difficulties. The first volume, entitled "Theological," dealt with the more fundamental groundwork of Theism; the present volume deals with the specific beliefs connected with the Person of Christ, while the third volume will be concerned with the Church; and it will be there that questions of authority and of what is meant by "Catholic," on which critics of the first volume have desired more light, will be considered. In the fourth volume subjects that can be generally summed up under the title "Eschatology" will be dealt with.

CONTENTS

	PAGE
THE PREPARATION FOR CHRIST	1
THE GOSPEL PORTRAIT OF CHRIST	17
THE CREDIBILITY OF THE GOSPELS	33
THE TEACHING OF JESUS	49
THE CONSCIOUSNESS OF CHRIST	65
THE DEATH OF JESUS	81
THE RESURRECTION	97
THE VIRGIN BIRTH	113
THE APOSTOLIC CHRISTOLOGY	129
THE CHRIST OF THE CREEDS	145
THE DOCTRINE OF THE TRINITY	161
THE DOCTRINE OF THE ATONEMENT	177

The following minor corrections need to be made in the present volume:

Page 4 (line 15) read *anything* instead of *no*.
Page 14 (line 19) read *domination* of Mithraism.
Page 24 (line 12) read *this* Gospel.
Page 57 (line 17) read *loved* instead of *had love*.
Page 65 (line 23) delete *to*.
Page 74 (line 1) read *as* the Disciples' Prayer.
Page 83 (line 27) insert *than* before to state.
Page 87 (last line but one) delete *that*.
Page 96 (line 8) read *conviction* instead of *convictions*.
Page 111 (line 26) read *but* instead of *which*.
Page 143 (line 11) delete *of*.
Page 192 (last par, line 1) delete *since*.

I

THE PREPARATION FOR CHRIST

CHRISTIANITY is a religion which took its rise from a previously existing religion, separated from it, and yet can never be properly understood apart from it. That religion was the religion of Israel, which is set forth authoritatively in the Old Testament Scriptures, less so in the Apocrypha, and still less in the recently recovered apocalyptic writings; though they are highly important because they bridge over the period between the Old and New Testament, and immediately precede and overlap the rise of Christianity. The Hebrew religion has continued and developed along its own line into modern Judaism, one of the world religions, whose distinctive continuance is, however, growing doubtful and whose attitude towards Christianity is likely to undergo considerable and perhaps dramatic change.

Its entanglement with the Hebrew religion is to some minds a great hindrance to Christianity; the binding up of the Old Testament with the New still misleads many readers into thinking that both stand on the same level of inspiration and authority; and many sectarian movements in Christianity, and not a few notions about God and His relations to men, are derived from Old Testament conceptions, in forgetfulness that they have been corrected and superseded by the Christian revelation. Sometimes the demand has been voiced that Christianity should be set free from its Hebrew

THE PREPARATION FOR CHRIST

grave-clothes, and this not only by radical thinkers in our revolutionary days, for quite early in the history of the Christian Church the Epistle of Barnabas maintained that the Jewish sacrificial system was not only merely a shadow of the good things to come, as the writer of the Epistle to the Hebrews also believed, but by a foolish misunderstanding on the part of the Jews, what was only meant to be a prophetic symbolism, had come to be practised as a rite. At a later period Marcion had carried the controversy with Judaism a stage further, and had rejected the Old Testament as containing a conception of God which must be distinguished as a quite other person than the God and Father of Jesus Christ, namely, the wicked demiurge or maker of the world; and in pursuance of his theory had eliminated from the New Testament all the writings which showed any favour or ascribed any truth to the older revelation. But apart from the fact that it would be almost impossible to understand the New Testament without continual reference to the Old, and that the New Testament continually appeals to Old Testament prophecies in proof that it is their fulfilment, and appropriates on behalf of the Church, as the New Israel, the promises made to the fathers, Jesus Himself, even when superseding the commands of the Law and selecting only certain prophetic teaching as in harmony with His own, undoubtedly acknowledged a divine revelation in the Old Testament; so that any drastic attempt to sunder the two covenants would not only leave us with a puzzle to which the clue was lost, but would seriously discredit the revelation claimed for the New Testament Scriptures themselves.

If, therefore, the Old Testament is to be taken as containing a revelation on which the New Testament builds, then we are faced with certain difficult questions: for instance, what kind of a revelation can that be which has to be in part corrected, supplemented and superseded; and if it is admitted that there is a true revelation of God contained in the Old Testament distinct from, and superior to, that which is found in other religions, or in the general religious ideas of humanity, why was this higher revelation confined to a single nation? These questions are not really dilemmas, but each can be answered in such a way that it clears away the difficulties inherent in the other. In the first place, the facts of Comparative Religion are sufficient to indicate two things: that a higher conception of God is found alongside the grossest superstitions, as if it were a survival of a purer faith; and that, whenever man sets himself, in response to the cravings of his own heart, to think out the meaning of life, he arrives at some conception of God which is not without a measure of comfort, truth and power. Now the religion of the Hebrews carries out both these processes on a higher level. Scholars can find in the Old Testament plenty of evidence not only for pre-existing, but for surviving pagan polytheism and heathen superstitions, and some would argue, therefore, that the emergence of ethical monotheism within Israel is due to nothing but a natural development instigated by the national experience of the Hebrews. It is a little difficult to understand how, on this hypothesis, a purely tribal God of a peculiarly exclusive nation came naturally to evolve into the idea of God as ethical, supreme and universal; whereas other religions, apparently starting from more philosophical conceptions, as in Hinduism, and with a consciously universal outlook, as in Buddhism, have failed to attain to the lofty conceptions of

THE PREPARATION FOR CHRIST

God's nature and personality found in the highest utterances of the Hebrew Scriptures. It is impossible to argue, as it once was argued, that the Semites have a natural tendency towards monotheism; the Babylonians never got far in this direction. It is only putting the question further back to attempt to trace the development of Israel's religion to the geographical home and the troubled history of the nation; for surely God uses both geography and history to train and educate mankind. The more Israel's religion is compared with other religions, the more we are compelled to posit a peculiar revelation made to this people. The exclusive spirit of the Jewish people, which prevented no more than the most minute and rarefied infiltration from other religions, the successful war of the prophets against heathen survivals and pagan corruptions, the triumphal progress of an ever purer faith, and especially the looking forward to a further revelation, which Christianity alone satisfies, are sufficient evidence that we must look here for some distinctive and supernatural revelation.

In the second place, when it is established that supernatural revelation is the only explanation of the superiority of the Hebrew religion, compared with what are called natural religions, then the question is raised why God, who by this religion is revealed to be universal and impartial in His concern and love for humanity, should have confined this revelation to one people and not have communicated it to all mankind. To answer this question is not easy; it necessitates the acceptance of a philosophy of history, it must assume the distinction between universal grace given to all men, and a higher grace which is only given as they respond to it sufficiently, and calls for some comprehension of the ultimate purposes of revelation. It is obviously the purpose of God to train men through fellowship one with another, and through their social experience, into a knowledge of Himself. All over the heathen world there have always been illuminated and saintly souls who have responded to the general grace given to all mankind, and who have thereby entered into a true knowledge of, and communion with, God; but they have remained isolated individual examples. The selection of a particular people and a peculiarly homogeneous nation was necessary in order that God should be conceived as related not only to individual souls, but in a way that involved not merely the communion of the soul with God, but faithful and fruitful fellowship with other souls. And therefore it is not merely interesting, it is highly instructive to note that it was only out of an intensely tribal religion that there came at last a universal idea of God, which at the same time maintained a vivid conception both of God and the religion He demands as personal. In order, therefore, for God to be fully revealed to all mankind, it was necessary for revelation to take this line; and the Old Testament Scriptures are sufficiently emphatic that the choice of Israel was not due to favouritism of any kind, but was solely that all the nations of the world should the sooner and surer come to the true knowledge of God.

Moreover, not only God's purpose, but man's need, calls for a revelation which is more than a mere communication of true ideas, for these are not satisfying to the human heart and not powerful enough to influence life. If God is going to reveal Himself to men with any sufficient certainty and adequate power, the revelation must be embodied

THE PREPARATION FOR CHRIST

in a personal character. It is for this perfect revelation that the whole history of Israel is a preparation. Whatever an incarnation may entail, it would be not only inconceivable, but impossible, without long previous preparation; it had to become the constant dream, the dominant expectation, and the central hope of a people. The moment this necessity is realized, all feeling of favouritism in the selection of the Jews vanishes. Reflecting upon the history of the Jews, and regarding that as a necessary part of God's revelation to them, the nations of the world might well wish to be exempt from any favour which took that form. The Jews had to be taught through humiliating disasters to abandon their dreams of a military empire; it was hammered out of them by a series of attacks, conquests and enslavements by the stronger nations which hemmed them round about, and this almost without cessation. Their constantly disturbed life on this restless plot of ground probably prevented absorption in philosophic thought, for which the Jewish mind has certainly proved its capacity, and their struggle against idolatry compelled them to sacrifice that delightful play of the human mind which finds expression in the plastic arts. We can discern in this isolation of interest a purpose that drove them first towards a perfect expression of the inspired word in their incomparable poetry, which has been such a source of strength and beauty to the languages that have fallen heir to their culture; but still more to the preparation for the Word becoming flesh, the conceiving within the womb of the nation not only of the body but of the rational soul, which, assumed by the Person of the Eternal Son, gave Jesus Christ to the world with all that He has meant for the revelation of God and the redemption of humanity.

THE PREPARATION FOR CHRIST

And not only did Israel have to pass through an almost perpetual history of chastening tribulation and heart-breaking disaster, but the emergence within this one nation of a pure idea of God was affected not by a general elevation of the conception among the common people, but through the exhortations of a series of prophets who had to struggle with the national consciousness against false conceptions of God and exclusive conceptions of its own destiny, with the common people against superstitious survivals, pagan syncretism and religious fickleness, and with compromising, faithless and cynical rulers; often in weary isolation, despite wholesale rejection, and sometimes rewarded only by persecution. We gain from this history some conception of the struggle that has to be waged by the Spirit of God with the spirit of man, since the bondage he has brought upon himself, before any true or worthy idea can gain acceptance by his mind and become embodied in his life.

The preparation for the coming of Christ is also clearly seen in the Hebrew conception of God as transcendent beyond all His created manifestations, as ethical to the point of a holiness exigent in its demands upon all who would approach Him and even dangerous where sin is rebelliously retained, and absolutely impartial whether in love, justice or mercy. This exalted conception of God, if it stood alone, would inevitably end in thrusting God at such a distance from man that his mind would doubt whether such a God really existed, and his heart despair whether he could ever enter into communion with Him. And so if God is to be accessible to men, He must reveal Himself in some way that, while doing nothing to deny His transcendence and His holiness, yet will make Him so familiar that He can dwell with man in spiritual friendship so

THE PREPARATION FOR CHRIST

affecting human personality by the pressure of His redeeming love that He can lift man beyond his sins and imperfections to Himself and to that heaven which He is and makes, and which can alone satisfy the heart of man, so infinitesimal and yet so touched with infinite desire.

In particular, Israel's religion prepares for Christ because of its anticipation of a Saviour. Despite the overwhelming conviction of the reality of God which dominated the prophetic consciousness; despite the sacrificial system of worship which secured common approach to God; and despite the communion with God reached by the Psalmists, the religion of the Old Testament is constantly conscious of man's need of a more convincing revelation of God, a greater assurance of forgiveness, and a higher type of communion.

In following out the prophecies of the Old Testament and their fulfilment in the New, we have to break away from the old-fashioned literalism which has been rendered impossible by more careful translations of the Old Testament predictions, as well as by the recognition that passages are often quoted in the New Testament with a meaning that the quoted passage in its context does not bear, and the original writer could not have intended; and we can do this the more easily because it involves an interpretation which has failed to convince the Jew and is too mechanical to satisfy the modern mind. At the same time, we must try to work towards the recognition of a far deeper, more spiritual and, in reality, a more miraculous fulfilment of the ancient prophecies, in that while the original writers often had something quite other in mind than the actual fulfilment in the life of Christ, the Old Testament is nevertheless full of hints and dreams and ideas which only the fulfilment lights

THE PREPARATION FOR CHRIST

up and brings out what was being groped after; while the vague and impersonal nature of all this shows how much more deeply the hope was really implanted than would be gathered from a mere selection of texts which were literally fulfilled in the career or summed up in the person of Christ. This newer reading of prophecy and its fulfilment can only be made clear by an exposition of the general hope by which Israel looked forward to a clearer revelation, a fuller salvation, and the establishment of a divine kingdom overruling all the kingdoms of the world.

Throughout the Old Testament we get the constant desire and expectation that God would manifest Himself to men in a way which would leave His reality and power unmistakable. This is often expressed in marvellous pictures of nature in its more terrible manifestations, when the ordinary course of things is broken through, as a veil rent in twain to disclose the grandeur behind God's creation; but this is evidently only symbolic of something that emerges into clearness when it is conceived that one day Jehovah Himself will stand upon the earth in some form which, however marvellous, shall be visible and tangible. The stories of theophanies as well as the longing for them illustrate this desire; but the flesh cries out for the living God, human eyes long to behold Him in some vision of the sanctuary, men crave some presence dwelling with them in familiar form, walking with them and being their God.

The more definite expression of this hope takes the form of the Messianic expectation. This expectation must not be confined to the single idea of some mighty deliverer or impressive personality, acting as the visible regent of the invisible God. This dominant person only forms a figure in the general picture of the reign of God manifested in a perfect theocracy, when all obey the Law of God written within their hearts, and in the extension of that recognized and obeyed sovereignty over the entire earth; attention converges on this figure only as it is discerned that the realization of this ideal could only come about through the agency of some mighty ruler and conqueror capable of establishing the kingdom and worthy of being regarded as in some sense an earthly viceroy of Jehovah. This form of the Messianic expectation naturally gathered to itself the idea of a great kingdom, and in combination with the ancient promise that the Davidic dynasty should never want a successor, concluded that the Messiah would be a son of David and his reign extend far beyond the confines of Palestine. But although Messiah's rulership is generally conceived as exercised through royal power, and the submission of the whole world is naturally imagined as brought about by military conquests, this is tempered by the idea that such a ruler must be motived by the love of justice, be a supreme lawgiver, and in his person manifest the wisdom which commends his rule to men; so that it is by his word rather than by his sword that he obtains universal dominion, by the law of peace rather than by the forceful repression of enemies that the nations are won to his allegiance, and he himself is so filled with the Spirit of God that he is as much a prophet as a king. As the need for social justice comes to be more felt, he is particularly thought of as a protector of the poor and possessed by a tender compassion for all in need, a man who is a refuge for men. Thus there is woven together the idea of might and mercy, of law and love, of power and personality, in a fashion which can only be understood when in the appearing of Christ we see what it is that is being groped after. Another combination is also gradually being constructed between the divine and the human: it is Jehovah Himself who is longed for, and yet it is an ever more human figure that is being conceived as necessary. A combination between the social and the personal conception is found later on in two impressive personifications of the ideal nation. The first of these is that known as the "Suffering Servant." It is generally agreed that this is a personification of the nation, as under the prophet's vision it is realized that the pious remnant of Israel has been suffering not for its own sins, but for the sins of the nation, and indeed for the sins of the whole world. The prophet rises to the idea that it is by vicarious suffering that the conscience of man is kept alive and the world is redeemed; and in interpreting the history of the true Israel in the light of this conception, he draws a picture which is so dramatically personified that it looks as if he had the career of some prophet or well-known martyr actually in mind. But the truth is we are dealing with a poetic creation that soars far beyond anything that can be historically interpreted of the nation or any member of it, and we have set before us an ideal person who by his self-offering becomes a sacrifice for sin. No one but Christ answers to this picture. The other personification is found in the vision of Daniel of one who comes with the clouds, is like unto a son of man, and is brought near to the ancient of days. There is no doubt that this is a personification of the humane kingdom which is to supersede and supplant the kingdoms more fitly symbolized by ferocious beasts. But here again the seer has allowed his personification to become so concrete that the impression remains of a person closely related to God as the only hope of establishing

THE PREPARATION FOR CHRIST

a divinely human kingdom on the earth. In the apocryphal Book of Enoch this figure becomes definitely a supernatural person, to whom is committed the judgment of the world. In this threefold combination of a human figure approaching the divine, a glorious conqueror who rules by his prophetic gifts, and a person who sums up social hopes and embodies the ideal of a theocratic kingdom, we have a mingling of elements whose meeting together could never have been foreseen, but are nevertheless perfectly combined in the personality, the character and the career of Christ.

Israel's expectations had not only taken this personal form, but her history had been moulded by unique personalities who were dominated by the word of the Lord. At first a prophetic utterance breaks forth from them in which the divine word almost displaces their own consciousness, for they see in visions and speak in ecstasy. Then this utterance of the word tends to become a possession by the Spirit of God, that manifests itself more in character than in speech. For finally we get a prophet like Hosea whose life and personality have a greater message than anything he can actually say; while in the prophet Jeremiah a conflict awakens between his personality and possession by the divine word: he resents the supersession of his own consciousness by the bursting forth of the prophetic word, which nevertheless he cannot suppress. We can see here a psychological preparation for a further revelation of God in personality; and it is obvious that if there is to be a fuller indwelling of the Spirit it must be by the Spirit of God supplanting the human personality and yet revealing itself not only as completely personal, but in nowise alien to anything proper to humanity. This movement the personality of Christ alone illuminates, by revealing what it was

THE PREPARATION FOR CHRIST

moving towards; and those who see in Jesus nothing more than a still further indwelling by the Spirit of God, another stage of elevation in the prophetic consciousness, ought on their own principles to recognize that any further development must produce an entirely new thing, namely, a combination of the human and the divine, where the Spirit of God completely occupies the place of the human person, and thereby creates a figure whose explanation must be supernatural and who at the centre of his personality is divine, but who is just as indisputably a natural and human personality. Therefore, in prophecy, in social expectation and in personal development, a place is being prepared which Christ, and Christ alone, most wonderfully fills. The prophetic prediction of minute details in Christ's career may be diminished by the extremest reduction that radical criticism may demand, and yet not only do there remain wonderful correspondences, as, for instance, between the picture of the Suffering Servant and the Passion of Christ, but a wider resemblance between prophecy and fulfilment comes into view in the general expectation and slowly manifesting social need and the movement towards the Kingdom of God inaugurated by Christ.

All this preparation is but a conscious development in one nation of a more widely spread though less clearly discerned movement in mankind as a whole. The study of the development of great religions like Hinduism and Buddhism shows how the human mind is groping after some idea of an incarnation of God in an historical person. In still vaguer fashion, we can find in primitive myths and in the mystery religions a similar expression of human craving for a communion with God that shall defy the weariness of life, survive the disaster of death, and initiate the soul into the secret of eternal life.

THE PREPARATION FOR CHRIST

The likeness in such movements, myths and mysteries to the slow conscious construction of Christian theology working upon the person and career of Christ cannot be explained, on the one hand, by reducing the historic figure of Jesus to a myth, nor, on the other, by the piling upon His person of a theology derived from other religions and philosophies, which His own utterances and consciousness do not necessitate; and, therefore, we have to see in them a farther spread, if fainter, prophecy which can be traced only to the Spirit of God working through the felt needs of the human heart and the free movement of the human mind. This world preparation was advancing to a pregnant stage just before the time of Christ. The Greek religion of the Olympian deities, although largely adopted by imperial Rome, was ceasing to satisfy popular need, and the mystery religions were everywhere becoming increasingly popular. In particular, the dominion of Mithraism was importing into the mysteries a moral seriousness which was not only preparing for the ethical message of Christianity, but because of that very seriousness was making men ready to abandon a mythology at the first touch, of a real historical, human figure, who could actually do for human nature what the mysteries had merely set forth in imaginative drama.

A great opportunity was being prepared in the widespread use of the Greek language which, in a debased, but simpler and more popular form, was providing a common language for the whole Empire. This was also familiarizing men with some of the conceptions of Greek philosophy; the idea of the Logos lay ready to hand, by which it was possible to interpret the meaning of Christ in terms of Platonic idealism. Philo, the Alexandrian Jew, had already taken in hand the task of interpreting the Hebrew

THE PREPARATION FOR CHRIST

theology in the terminology of Plato; and, whether by direct borrowing, or by the general spread of such ideas, some of his phrases concerning the Logos are found in the New Testament applied to Christ. The Roman rule had for the time being brought peace to the western world; the great roads that ran from the furthest confines of the Empire to Rome were arteries along which any good news could travel, while the perpetual movement of Roman soldiers and officials with their large retinue of slaves and traders made it impossible for anything which happened in any corner of the Empire to remain long unknown. Nevertheless, this Roman peace was leaving a great deal to be desired: there was something repressing and unnatural about it; it was being accompanied by a sad deterioration in the old Roman morality, and the most serious-minded thinkers knew something more was needed. Virgil had been seeking to exalt the honour of the Julian family, who had founded the Empire, by tracing their divine descent, and had predicted the birth of some heaven-sent descendant of their line in a fashion which is so reminiscent of the Isaianic expectation of the Messiah that it is felt by many students that he must have been acquainted with the Hebrew Scriptures. This is probably unnecessary; but there had been a considerable attraction towards the Jewish religion felt by Greeks and Romans, many of whom had become proselytes, and this must have made the Messianic hope something more than a national expectation and the secret of a peculiar people. Throughout Palestine itself, the publishing of apocalyptic works and the irritation under Roman rule had combined to revive the expectation of a Messiah to fever heat, and although it had inevitably taken a military form in the minds of the more violent revolutionists, there was a remnant among the poor and meek who were

THE PREPARATION FOR CHRIST

looking for something more essentially religious, and yet no less an answer to the cry for social and political deliverance. It was into this world, athrob with expectation, prepared both materially and spiritually for the word to run swiftly, eager for good news of God and anxious for an assurance of immortality, that Christ was born.

II

THE GOSPEL PORTRAIT OF CHRIST

THERE stepped on to the stage of human history somewhere about the beginning of our era (which indeed dates itself from His birth, though not with sufficient accuracy, for He was probably born about B.C. 6), the figure to whom was given the name of Jesus Christ; named Jesus by His parents, in obedience to a heavenly direction and as an indication of His mission, and Christ by His followers, in the belief that He was the promised Messiah of the Jews. The forces set in movement in history by the appearance of that person; whether in the interior religious experience of His worshippers, by whom He is regarded as a living presence in the heart; in the institution of the Christian Church, which claims to be an organization governed by His Spirit; or in His wider influence upon the course of civilization and the developing thought of man, are indisputable, immense and increasing. For although the significance and explanation of His appearance have become in modern times, through the questioning of the position given to Christ by the Church, a matter of widespread discussion and widely divergent opinion, at least He continues to be the most discussed person in history. Christ may be disliked or denied; He cannot be ignored or left alone. Opposition to His claims was aroused during His lifetime, and to such an extent that it led to His violent death; and that opposition naturally continues, but at different stages and in such constant flux and instability, that the tendency is discernibly either towards such a rejection of Christ as implicitly involves the rejection of any revelation, opposition to all religion, and complete pessimism about the capacity of the human mind for truth, the future of our race and the meaning of existence, or to the acceptance of Christ by the mind as the revelation of the essential nature of God, by the heart as the only solution of the problem of personality, by society as the one hope of human redemption. Through all changes of thought, past all social and political revolutions, and still far ahead of the undoubted ethical progress of the race, Christ perpetually challenges the mind with His own question as to who He is and how He is to be thought of, and the world to accept Him as its Lord and King, or decree its own destruction.

It is impossible to evade this challenge on the excuse that the Jewish Messianic hope brought forward many claimants, that other religions had founders who also exercised and claimed to reveal the secret of life or the will of God, and who still exercise a mysterious influence over their followers, and that the world has never been without a succession of those who have claimed that they had a plan which, if accepted, would save human society. For no one but Christ has ever claimed, and had claimed for Him, at one and the same time, that He was the Son of God, as such had unique knowledge of the Divine nature and purpose, and could therefore convey salvation to the individual soul and to the whole world. The claims of Christ have therefore to be accepted for what they are, or completely rejected, with the inevitable corollary that Christ was an imposter or an ego-maniac; or an attempt must be made to explain these claims as an exaggeration on the part of His followers, which must

THE GOSPEL PORTRAIT OF CHRIST

involve the adoption of some theory of Christian origins about which there is no prospect of proof or agreement; while if Christ's claims are accepted as true, this must involve some theory of incarnation, some theory of a Church originally commissioned and constantly inspired by Him, and some theory of salvation, both of the individual soul and of human society, which depends upon this acceptance of His claims.

Faced with these issues, whether merely to discuss Christ's significance, or to reject or accept His claims, we naturally turn to the four short records of His life known as the Gospels, in order to determine what He claimed to be, whether His teaching supports these claims, and whether the general impression of His personality upon those about Him is at all congruous with such claims. This must entail a prolonged enquiry; but our immediate concern is with the impression made upon His contemporaries, especially upon His immediate followers, and particularly upon the writers of the four Gospels, in order to discover who and what Jesus Christ must be believed to be.

In approaching the Gospels in order to recover the portrait, and behind the portrait the living figure of Christ, we must keep certain considerations in mind. The Gospels are not the earliest documents about Christ; their literary publication was certainly preceded by some of the Epistles of St. Paul. This important fact has two bearings; firstly, those Epistles presuppose that the main outlines of the Gospel story are already known, and assume that the significance given to Christ by the Apostle's teaching is supported by the character, the teaching and the career of Christ; secondly, the Gospels were written by men, and probably for men, who held the Apostle's opinion about Christ. This means that the Gospels cannot be isolated from the theological atmosphere in which they were composed without distorting their full meaning. Further, if Christ is an ever-living Spirit really in touch with the hearts of His worshippers and, in some analogical fashion, the Church continues His incarnation, then He is also known by spiritual means, and known all the surer as the period when He lived on earth recedes into the past. But this is a claim which obviously must be tested by what can be ascertained from His actual utterances during His earthly lifetime; and whether it be mystical experience or ecclesiastical doctrine, it will be admitted by all who maintain their continuous and illuminating contribution, that these must be related to the facts and teaching of the Gospels, even if only as a developing doctrine is related to its creative idea, or a full-grown tree to its root and seed.

When, however, we turn to the Gospels in order to see what kind of personality is there presented to us, we are faced with the discovery that the Gospels are not so much biographies as contain the materials for a biography. Moreover, the ground covered in the four biographies is slightly different in the first three and considerably different in the fourth. This difference creates certain difficulties and raises certain questions, not all of which have found adequate solution or sufficient explanation. It is obvious from the composition of any single one of them that they each comprise only a selection, and no one of the authors has set out to write a full life of Jesus. But while the selection according to St. Mark is on the whole retained by the authors of the Gospels according to St. Matthew and according to St. Luke, even down to the order of events and the actual words of the narrative, and their own material is simply added thereto, the Gospel accord-

THE GOSPEL PORTRAIT OF CHRIST

ing to St. John strikes out an entirely new line; its order is quite different, and the diction seems to have undergone a complete change. But even this last Gospel does not attempt a full life, but obviously assumes that the other three Gospels were already known, and distinctly states that an abundance of material remains unchronicled. In addition, when we try to penetrate beyond these portraits, partly copied from one another, to the original, we are obviously setting ourselves a difficult and, unless a certain fidelity can be assumed, an indecisive task: to cancel out the personal equation of the painter in order to gain our own impression of the personality portrayed. Now in the first three Gospels it is obvious that the writers allow their own personality very little play; their method is extraordinarily objective, they seem so dominated by their subject that they are content merely to record what Christ said or did, and how people around Him reacted; and almost their only influence upon the narrative seems to have been that of selection. But the author of the Fourth Gospel, on the other hand, is obviously a person of profound mentality; the diction of the Gospel is so consistently his own that we cannot always be sure whether he is reporting an utterance or making his own comments. In the first three Gospels there is no overt attempt to call the reader's attention to any important or significant point; and only in the fourth is there sometimes given a clue to motive or purpose, and then not always when we most feel the need of it. The Gospels are written without exclamation marks, italics or the copious psychological explanations of modern biographies, and the reader is therefore thrown back upon his own surmises; and unless he has recourse to the apostolic faith concerning Christ he might sometimes be at a complete loss as to the meaning of some utterances or the purpose of some incident, if not almost at a loss as to why the Gospel story was written.

Take for instance the Gospel of St. Mark; if it be read through swiftly and yet carefully, so that a general impression may be gained, it suggests not only an obviously selected, incomplete and even a compressed and hurried story, but if it were taken alone and no other sources for the life of Christ were available, it would be almost unintelligible; not that it does not contain hints about Christ's person to which the other Gospels, the Epistles, and indeed the Church's full faith alone give any adequate explanation, and in addition its dramatic swiftness and decisive movements, even though often unexplained, manage to convey an impression of profound importance and most critical significance. The additional material in the Gospels according to St. Matthew and St. Luke do not add any noticeably different colouring to the Marcan outline, save that the teaching in St. Matthew is more concerned with the relation towards the old religion and, though more slightly, with the ecclesiastical provision for handing on the new; the teaching in St. Luke is specially marked by tenderness and sympathy, especially with sinners, women and the poor; while in the Fourth Gospel, on the other hand, the actual time setting is extended, the motion is slow, the sayings are reiterated and further expounded, and arguments concerning Christ's person and mission are threshed out to final issues. The four Gospels thus taken together do gradually not only enrich the material, but reveal its meaning.

Before the rise of modern criticism little difficulty was felt in the differences between the first three Gospels and the fourth on the one hand, or between the general gospel portrait and the apostolic theology on the other, or, still further, between all these and the formulated ecclesiastical doctrine and the mystical experience of Christ in the hearts of the saints. If it was a composite portrait the various elements seemed to be complementary and the whole to be consistent; whereas now not only has this resultant portrait been declared to have been painted over by different hands, but layer after layer has been removed under the belief that only thus can we recover the original portrait, and then safely infer what the subject Himself actually looked like. It is commonly declared that criticism has restored to us the historical Jesus, and it is assumed that this process is not only legitimate, but necessary if we are to come face to face with Jesus as He actually was. That criticism has almost certainly determined the order in which the Gospels were written, and the measure of their literary dependence upon one another, may with fair safety be assumed; that the microscopical investigation of the Gospels has drawn attention to important details which were liable to be overlooked in the general view will be gratefully acknowledged; that this perpetual poring over the Gospels has produced in the minds of students a sense of the historical reality and profound significance of the person, the life and the teaching of Jesus may in some cases be admitted; and this may be one reason why His figure stands clearer and more arrestingly before our century than perhaps to any previous one save that in which He actually lived. But that criticism has recovered the historical Jesus buried beneath the Gospels, to reach which we have to disregard whole Gospels like the fourth, many passages in St. Luke, St. Matthew, and even items in St. Mark as unhistorical and untrue to the original, is very gravely to be questioned; and for reasons which must now be set forth.

THE GOSPEL PORTRAIT OF CHRIST

The agreed and authoritative canons of historical criticism are in great need of being set forth and carefully examined for their general validity, and for their special application to the problem of the Gospels, before we can allow conclusions to be drawn as to what may be regarded as original and historical and what must be ruled out as later addition, legendary growth, or sheer invention. The mere fact that a Gospel comes earliest in time does not of itself determine its superior historicity; there may have been a selective purpose at work, and just because their Gospel was early, many things may have been omitted because they would be well known; and as the living memory of Jesus receded, later Gospels would have to substitute this by supplementary details. The emergence of various questions concerning Christ might well serve to recall what He had said, which previously had seemed unimportant or unintelligible, or had been entirely forgotten, and need not simply be suspected of giving rise to sayings and events invented to meet the situation. The rejection of certain sayings or incidents because they seem to be inconsistent with others demands a very patient and informed investigation as to what is really inconsistent with so wide and original a character as that of Jesus. We cannot here set forth the principles of a valid criticism and then apply them in detail to the Gospel, but it may be said in general, without much fear of disproof, that it is impossible by any legitimate critical method to reduce the Gospel portrait to a historic original, which does not still give rise to the questions to which, in varying degree, Christ's own self-disclosure, the apostolic theology and Church doctrine are the only adequate answers forthcoming.

For instance, if the Gospel of St. Mark be taken

THE GOSPEL PORTRAIT OF CHRIST

as so regulative that anything that adds to it something further by way of claim, revelation or reverence must be ruled out, we are still left not only with the insistent problem of the person and mission of Jesus facing us, but with sufficient hints in that Gospel alone as to what the solution is. We have the picture of a dominating and powerful personality creating the most intense and widespread amazement at the authority of His teaching and at His mighty works. At the very outset of the story we are faced with a person who claims that He has the power to forgive sins, a power which the disputants declare belongs to God alone, whom He only answers by showing that nevertheless it is possessed by Himself. Soon after, Jesus claims the right to determine how far He shall obey the rigidly observed and divinely appointed ordinance of the Sabbath, because even this is a matter over which He is supreme. His power over the wind and the sea is manifested in such an extraordinary fashion that His disciples break out into the question, which really underlies and pervades this whole Gospel: " Who then is this ? " He starts an argument with the Scribes as to how one whom David calls Lord can be his son ; the point of which is not to dispute the Davidic lineage of the Messiah, but to raise the question whether one who is honoured by so high a name can be merely the descendant of a human king. The movement of the Gospel hurries Jesus to the final conflict without much indication as to what brought it about ; but His condemnation is on the charge of blasphemy for claiming to be something He had no right to claim, which would not be mere Messiahship, but that as involving some divine relationship. This complicated issue is submitted to by Jesus on His own explanations that He came to fulfil the Scriptures and give His life as a ransom. These are sufficient instances that even in the earliest Gospel Christ's personality raises the problem of His divine relationship and redemptive mission.

The endeavour has been made to go behind the earliest Gospel and, by picking out certain sayings of Christ which seem directly to conflict with the Church's belief concerning Him, to discredit the latter as contrary to Christ's own teaching. Two such sayings may be instanced from St. Mark's Gospel. One is Christ's sharp pulling up of the young man, who saluted Him as " good master," with the declaration that no one was good save God; and this is taken to be an implicit denial by Christ that He was divine. But apart from the contradiction to other claims that this would involve, there are three possible explanations of this saying: that Christ denied His own goodness, which would be little better than mock modesty; or that He declared all goodness was derived from God, which would be a mere platitude; or that the young man must either desist from empty compliments or find a theological sanction for them. This last must be the meaning, because in telling His questioner how to obtain eternal life Christ puts the following of Himself in place of the first half of the Decalogue which sets forth man's duty to God. The second saying is the cry of dereliction on the Cross. This saying cannot be taken to indicate that Christ died in despair because God had not come to His rescue, for this would be in complete contradiction to many expressed expectations that He would be crucified and put to death. In addition, the fact that the words are a quotation and were uttered under the torture of an agonizing death, forbids any such explanation; but however mysterious that cry must remain, it at least assumes some wonderfully

THE GOSPEL PORTRAIT OF CHRIST

close relationship with God as normal to Christ's consciousness.

Every effort to reduce the Gospel portrait to that of a purely human figure is doomed to failure, for the irreducible minimum always contains material which demands a maximum explanation. A radically reductive criticism must always fail; for to reduce the figure of Jesus to something quite undistinguished and unexceptional would not even explain the subsequent growth of legend and exaggeration. And the attempts to construct an intelligible picture on the remains which radical criticism would leave us have proved so entirely contradictory that they are sufficient to indicate that a great deal of this criticism is purely subjective and arbitrary. It is only necessary to recall the utterly divergent reconstructions of the "historic" Jesus which have superseded and cancelled one another.

It used to be the custom among radical critics to picture Jesus as a mere teacher of a purely interior religion, of which He was at most an example, but in no sense its object, inculcating the adoption of His own attitude to the Father as that which was universally true of the soul, or attainable by all men. On this basis it was doubted whether Jesus regarded Himself as the Messiah, any saying which claims that Christ has a unique relationship to the Father was rejected, and it overlooked the significance of the important, because indirect, evidence that Jesus never refers to God as "our Father," save in the prayer which, although called the Lord's Prayer, He Himself only taught others to pray. But this picture has been completely discredited by the later one which imagines Jesus obsessed by apocalyptic ideas, believing in a catastrophic coming of a purely supernatural order which He Himself was sent to proclaim and set in motion. This picture has to rule out all reference to the Kingdom of God as an interior experience and a present possession, and although it conceives Jesus as dominated by the Messianic idea and conscious of Himself as the pre-existing and supernatural Son of Man, it leaves the impression of a fanatical figure who was moreover completely disappointed in His expectations. Again, the portrait of Christ as an individualistic revolutionary has naturally gained considerable acceptance in recent years. This conceives Christ as in rebellion against the prevailing conception of God, the external observance of religion and all the conventions of piety; picturing Him almost as a sort of Prometheus at war with any God save the God within. But to establish this picture as genuine, all sayings have to be rejected in which the Old Testament teaching is appealed to as still authoritative; His own observance of the accepted ritual has to be ignored, His cleansing of the Temple, which He evidently regarded as too sacred to be commercialized or secularized, as well as the teaching which shows that, while He regarded as the grossest hypocrisy the substitution of external observance for social justice and personal duty, He never proposed that if the one was done the other might be left undone. On the other hand, if Christ's attitude towards the Old Testament revelation and the external observance of religion is to be made intelligible, it is inconceivable that He should not have made provision for the carrying on of a purified religion by responsible persons who accepted His teaching, such as we actually find He did provide for in His commissioning of the Apostles and the institution of the Eucharist. Still more impossible is the attempt to make Christ a teacher of pure humanitarian ethics into which there must be no intrusion of His own claims as the inspiring motive as well as the ultimate object of ethical behaviour, but which disregards all objective religion whatsoever as separable from His ethical teaching, whose independence enables it to stand alone; for the two are so woven together that any attempt to unravel them would leave the Gospels in tatters. The impression of His character, reconstructed on this critical basis, runs out to similar extremes and contradictions: on the one hand Christ is regarded as an utterly passive and submissive teacher of meekness, non-resistance and withdrawal from life as the only solution of its personal and social problems; and then this is dismissed as completely untrue, and in its place there is portrayed a person of such violent words and deeds that it is only natural that He made bitter enemies, whose only course, if they wanted to retain their self-respect or preserve the stability of society, was to put Him out of the way.

It must not be assumed, however, that nothing has been gained by modern criticism, even if it had left us only impressionist sketches of Christ which are hurried, arbitrary and perverse; for they have served to call attention to often neglected aspects and to reveal to us the extraordinary richness and complexity of the material which the Gospels contain. But evidently, to paint a life-like portrait of Jesus, or, still more, to sculpture Him in the round, to see both His wholeness and consistency, is at present almost beyond us; and yet in Himself there is no indication of confusion or consciousness of inconsistency; the impression remains of a completely unified personality, which nothing was able to break up, with a single purpose which neither rejection nor death was able to deflect. It seems therefore as if we ought to attempt a more life-like portrait of Christ by taking the material of the Gospels as a whole, and not hurriedly resorting to the rejection of details which we find difficult or which seem to us inconsistent; for hardly two persons can be found who are agreed as to what details must be so rejected; nor are we under any obligation to accept conclusions drawn from a criticism whose canons have not been themselves sufficiently criticized, and which has led to such contradictions and confusion.

If we are to attempt the task at which criticism has failed, it can only be done by seeking to combine and resolve the apparent oppositions which are felt to exist. *First* of all, the Jesus of the Gospels is obviously a mysterious figure; it is not only that the stories of His entrance into this life and of His exit from it are in the highest degree supernatural, but His own references to His coming and His going are full of a sense of mystery; He does not speak as one who finds Himself in this world and then chooses a vocation; He is conscious of being sent into this world on a pre-determined mission. And if He is to be hurried out of it by the violent action of His enemies, He declares that He will remain a judge of all subsequent events, and all history will be a process by which He comes back again. It sometimes looks as if Jesus was unaware of who He was, not only because He asks others who they think Him to be, but because He seems to be searching round in the Old Testament for titles and prophecies of Himself in order to describe who He is and to confirm His own sense of His mission. But the fact that he combines the title of the "Son of Man" with the idea of the "Suffering Servant"; that He dislikes, because of its political associations, the title

THE GOSPEL PORTRAIT OF CHRIST

" Son of David " or " the Christ," yet will deny neither; and that He prefers to elicit from others the confession of what He is, and at St. Peter's confession professes Himself satisfied, is rather a sign that He knew all along who He was, but that to reveal this prematurely to others would prejudice judgment and might cheapen loyalty. Nor does there seem much real evidence that He only gradually awoke to His mission or to His identity; as soon as ever He was conscious of Himself He was conscious of His Father, and from the very outset of His mission He was clear as to how it was to end. It may be a difficulty for our modern conceptions, but the fact cannot be ignored, can hardly have been invented, and has never been explained away, that there was a set of persons, namely the demon-possessed, who at once recognized Jesus for what He was. In the *second* place, Christ manifested extraordinary might, not only over evil forces in nature, such as the sickness and diseases which plague men, but also over its normal operations; for there is no kind of criticism that can drive a wedge between the healing and the " nature " miracles, or can reduce His healing powers to the mere " suggestion " of modern mental therapeutics. And yet, at the end, when His enemies fell upon Him, He was utterly helpless. The only explanation of this must be a moral and spiritual one: namely, that the powers which He possessed He believed He ought to use only for others, and that since the only alternative to His submission to death would be to resist by armed violence, he regarded His death as a necessary means of ransoming men from sin and delusion. In the *third* place, we have a curious combination in the authority with which He corrected the Old Law, issued commands and stated truth, while at the same time

He appealed for the acceptance of His teaching, not on the basis of His mere statement, but upon its examination and acceptance only if found true by the reason and the conscience of His hearers. *Fourth:* while His whole ethical teaching is the advocacy of the way of love rather than the way of violence, both His words and His actions are of the most violent kind; and the solution of this is that His compassion and love for men were so violent that they were liable to be mistaken for ordinary passion and anger. *Fifth:* we must keep together two facts: that He claimed a unique relationship to His Father, and also that He came into the world to invite men to share that relationship by believing on Him.

Now there is no really intelligible reconciliation of these various oppositions, for which we must somehow find room, unless we are going to tear the Gospels in half at the dictation of a one-sided consistency, or in mere impatience with the problem, save in the full and final portrait of Jesus as a divine Being who has become man in order to lift men to the divine life; His teaching, His life and His death being the means of bringing about this union, proclaiming and making certain the forgiveness of God, destroying the power of sin, and the attraction of His love winning men to accept His Father as their own. It is this portrait that Catholic theology paints: the materials are provided by the Gospels; and these materials are derived from the teaching, the works and the life of the historic Jesus.

III

THE CREDIBILITY OF THE GOSPELS

THE four Gospels may be regarded as presenting us with materials for the construction of a life of Jesus, or as a series of sketches from which we may gather the nature and significance of His personality. Yet to write a historical life of Jesus or to paint a portrait which will convey all this to the modern mind has proved a well-nigh impossible task. There is first of all the necessity of fitting in the life of Jesus with the history of His times. Then there are gaps in the Gospel material and incidents which need further explanation; details found in one Gospel appear to conflict with details found in another; and not only does the Fourth Gospel contain material widely differing from that found in the Synoptics, but it gives a widely different presentation of Christ, of which everyone must be aware, and which some feel to be irreconcilable with the presentation in the Synoptics.

Modern criticism, which has nevertheless attempted this task of setting forth the historical Jesus, proceeds upon the general principle of comparing first one Gospel with another, then the record of the words of Christ with the record of His works, and finally of one saying with another; and on this basis would eliminate anything that looks like inconsistency, exaggeration and later accretion. While it is obvious that comparison is legitimate and is invited by the very nature of the material presented to us, the way in which the process has been applied, and the conclusions that have been erected thereon, have led to almost everything in the Gospels being questioned : nothing seems left on which we can build with certainty ; so that to write a historic life of Christ appears impossible, and it has even been doubted whether the Gospel story has any historical basis whatever. These disappointing and destructive conclusions may, however, be due to faulty principles or to their misapplication ; and we are driven to suspect the influence of historical theories and philosophical presuppositions which are alien to strictly critical principles, and the intrusion into critical conclusions of what are mere guesses and baseless speculations.

The contradictory conclusions to which the professed application of the same critical principles have led have been previously summarized, but for our present purpose we need only draw attention to two, whose complete opposition is significant and instructive. The one is the conclusion that the historical origin of the Gospel story was a purely human figure who never claimed to be in any way different from the rest of mankind ; the other is the conclusion that the original of the Gospel story was a myth of a divine being who never had any historical existence. Now it is evident that the Pauline Epistles present us with a conception of Christ as the divine Son of God, who pre-existed before His human life in a state of glory, and relinquished that state in order to bring to earth the message of salvation and open a way by which mankind could come to God. Therefore the Pauline theology must have completely obscured the original Gospel and transfigured the human personality of Jesus ; and this process was carried to completion within thirty years of the Crucifixion. It is held, however, that the Gospels so faithfully reproduce the original historical basis of Christianity, that we are compelled to admit that such a transformation has actually taken place. But before this contention can be established two grave objections have to be met. The first is that while the Pauline Epistles betray the fact that serious differences of opinion at one time existed between the Apostle Paul and the original Apostles, and that while St. Paul's authority and teaching were sometimes challenged and questioned by other teachers, by opponents, and by his own converts, never once is there any hint that there was any difference of opinion about his conception of Christ's personality and significance. And the other difficulty is that the whole tenor of the Fourth Gospel and many sayings in the Synoptics support the Pauline conception; and this difficulty can only be overcome by dismissing the Fourth Gospel as unhistorical and regarding many passages in the Synoptics as misunderstanding on the part of the evangelists, adaptations due to developing opinion, or subsequent interpolations. But not only is there considerable disagreement among critics as to whether the Fourth Gospel must be regarded as sheer romance or as having some historical basis, there is no agreement whatever as to what passages of the Synoptics are to be excised as unhistorical or tendencious; while the endeavour to eliminate everything from the four Gospels which ascribes to Christ supernatural power or to His Person supernatural significance would lead to complete disintegration of the Gospels, and would reduce their central figure to such dimensions that it would be difficult to see why such accretions should ever have gathered about His name. It is impossible not to think that a great deal of this criticism is dominated by philosophical prejudices against the supernatural and also by the modern theory of evolution, which is

THE CREDIBILITY OF THE GOSPELS

here applied in an uncritical fashion. For on a purely chronological sequence we get first the Epistles, with their advanced theological conceptions, then come the Synoptic Gospels, the original outline of which is supposed to be free from these conceptions, and then these again accumulate until they are embodied in the Fourth Gospel, which, although rising to claim a significance for Christ as high as that made by the Pauline theology, does so by a quite different route, and expresses itself in entirely different terms.

The other and entirely opposite conclusion to which we have referred must now be examined. It has been reached by another school and has been encouraged by the extravagances and confusions which the purely humanitarian interpretation has produced, and has consequently run to the other extreme, claiming that, whether with or without any reduction of their material, the Gospels consistently picture a being who speaks and acts and is conceived as divine; and since the notion of a divine being becoming human and appearing in history is held to be inconceivable, there are only two conclusions open, one that Jesus was deluded, and the other that the whole Gospel story is a myth. An examination of the former of these alternative hypotheses must for the present be postponed; and although the theory that Christ is a myth has failed to secure even consideration from recognized experts in New Testament criticism and history, a few worthless and yet pretentious books have gained a certain currency amongst uncritical readers, and if the presentation of Christianity is to obtain a hearing from everyone and is to proceed along a sure road, we must remove the last possibility of any suspicion that the Gospel story is without historical basis.

The exponents of the myth hypothesis appeal first of all to the silence of contemporary history

THE CREDIBILITY OF THE GOSPELS

concerning Jesus, though there is nothing remarkable in the actual facts. Christianity begins to be mentioned in pagan history just when that might be expected, namely in the *Annals of Tacitus*, written about the year A.D. 100. The silence of Josephus, the Jewish historian, writing about ten years earlier, constitutes an apparent difficulty; but first of all it is not a complete silence, for even if the one longer passage which refers to Christ is a forgery, the sentence referring to " the brother of Jesus, the so-called Christ, whose name was James," cannot be questioned; and even the longer passage is now defended by competent scholars as at least only expanded from some short reference which would be more natural to find in Josephus; for he obviously not only did not believe in Christ, but was anxious to conceal the Messianic expectations of the Jews in order to ingratiate himself with the Roman authorities. Moreover, the argument from silence, always dangerous in a case like this, has to refuse without warrant the witness of the rest of the New Testament literature, and in particular the early Epistles of St. Paul. Further, this hypothesis has to explain how such a myth arose, and then there are produced two alternatives which cannot both be true. The one is that the whole Gospel story is due to the writing up of Old Testament prophecies into a historic narrative. Now while it is possible that here and there the New Testament narrative may have been slightly adapted in order to make the fulfilling of a prophecy more dramatic and detailed, and while Old Testament prophecies are quoted which were never taken to be Messianic by the Jews, and to a modern reader have nothing to do with a prediction of the Gospel story, it would be nothing less than a literary miracle to take these scattered references, whose prophetic meaning could never even be discerned until some historical event had called them to mind, and piece them together so as to construct this marvellous story. The other explanation is that the Gospels are an adaptation of pagan and heathen myths; but this involves such ludicrous identifications of persons and events with these ancient myths, and so overlooks the almost fanatic hostility of the Jews to the whole realm of pagan thought, that it deserves even less consideration. Moreover, neither of these alternative hypotheses does anything to account for the mass of wonderful sayings attributed to Jesus, which have such an unmistakable style, penetrating outlook and consistent philosophy as to make it impossible that they should have been collected together from different sources; while if they were the invention of one mind, that mind itself would have to be proclaimed one of the greatest spiritual geniuses that humanity had ever produced; and how and by what stages this myth came to be believed in as veritable history no one can tell us, and the process is indeed unthinkable. The myth hypothesis may therefore be dismissed as critically, historically and psychologically impossible.

The mere rejection of the two extreme theories that the Gospels can be wholly reduced by a process of criticism to a purely human figure who has been gradually transformed into a divine being, or to the unhistorical myth of a divine being who has been gradually transformed into an historical figure, nevertheless does not tell us what the historical basis of the Gospels is, or how far we may take the Gospels to be trustworthy; and, unfortunately, in the present state of criticism, we cannot appeal to critical conclusions to answer these questions, because there is no sort of agreement amongst the critics to which we can refer as sufficiently authoritative for this purpose. But we are not therefore left without any possibility of establishing the credibility of the Gospels; indeed, from the very facts to which the most radical criticism has called attention it is possible to build up a series of valid arguments which go to prove the credibility of the Gospels; and this we shall now attempt.

It must be borne in mind, however, that we are not going to attempt to demonstrate the *historicity* of the Gospels, for, in face of modern scepticism, to prove even that Jesus was a historic person would be impossible; not because there are real grounds for doubting it, for it is as certain as any historical fact can be, but the results of a century of historical criticism and the persistent insinuations of religious scepticism have left the modern mind almost without the capacity for trusting traditions that are inherently trustworthy, and with a natural tendency to question any historic fact which has been made of religious importance. We have to wait for a gradual change of temper, which the rehabilitation of tradition and the discrediting of a radical criticism that has produced only negative and contradictory results is slowly bringing about. Moreover, we are not attempting the impossible task, for indeed there is no means open to historical science, of establishing the truth of any and every event in the Gospels which anyone may feel inclined to question. Ours is a much more modest task, namely to show that the Gospels are *credible*; that is, that it is reasonable to believe that they are on the whole and in detail sufficiently trustworthy accounts of what actually happened. This trustworthiness

THE CREDIBILITY OF THE GOSPELS

is called for by the general consistency of the Gospels, the obvious seriousness and certainty of the writers regarding facts which they believe to be of the profoundest significance for the salvation of humanity; by the necessity for positing the Gospel story as a fact in order to account for the happenings immediate, continuous and progressive to which it has given rise; and by the impossibility of suggesting any historical, psychological or sociological process by which any origin other than that recorded could have produced the Gospel story or accounted for the rise of the Christian Church.

Now the first point to which radical criticism has called attention that we may regard as containing positive evidence for the credibility of the Gospels is the great difference between the theology of the Pauline Epistles and the religious teaching of the Gospels. We shall show at a later stage that the Pauline theology is not an illegitimate development, indeed an inevitable one, and the only possible explanation of the Gospel story. But everyone would admit that it is a development, that it has a different emphasis and a profoundly different terminology. But while the Gospels were almost certainly written later than the earliest Epistles of St. Paul, they definitely reflect an earlier stage of religious thought and an entirely different historical setting. They are closely related to a complex, peculiar and contemporary history; and while, on looking back, we may be able to see that the translation of Christ's teaching and the impression made by His Person into the Pauline theology was a natural and necessary development, no one with only the Pauline Epistles before them could have constructed a life of Christ such as the Gospels show, or in order to provide the Pauline Gospel with a

THE CREDIBILITY OF THE GOSPELS

historical basis would have painted such a picture of Christ as the Gospels portray. Radical criticism has first used the Gospels to show that the Pauline theology is an illegitimate development, and then, finding the Pauline theology anticipated in the Gospels, used this to discredit their historicity. The two processes negative each other, and the only true conclusion from the actual facts pointed out is one that establishes the historicity of the Gospels and the validity of the Pauline theology; for not only do the Gospels contain the germ of the Pauline theology, but the Epistles of St. Paul contain sufficient references to the life, the personality, the teaching of Jesus to show that St. Paul was aware of and built upon the facts recorded in the Gospels. From the accepted authenticity and early date of the Pauline Epistles we may therefore argue to the historicity of the Gospels.

Another set of facts to which attention has been drawn by radical criticism is the apparent inconsistency of certain statements in the Gospels when compared with their obvious general purpose to present us with the picture of a divine being living on earth. These facts can be shown to be not inconsistent with such a purpose, for they are capable of reconciliation with it, and if they had not been would not have been admitted by the writers; but the *apparent* difference does show that these statements at any rate have not been invented and were only put in because they happened. For instance: in view of St. Mark's representation of Christ as a worker of mighty miracles, it would never have been stated that " He could there do no mighty works because of their unbelief," unless it was a fact; in view of St. Matthew's representation of our Lord as possessing intimate knowledge of the Father as His Son, he would never have stated that "of that day and hour knoweth no one, not even the angels of heaven, neither the Son, but the Father only," unless Jesus had said it; according to that same Gospel, seeing that Jesus had stated that if He asked for it His Father would send more than twelve legions of angels for His protection, to go on to record that on the cross Jesus said, "My God, my God, why hast thou forsaken me?" is a proof that He did say it. Many other similar sayings might be quoted which appear to be so out of accord with the general presentation of the Gospels that we can be certain at least that these are facts. A distinguished radical critic has collected a number of these, which he has called "Foundation Pillars," and it has been hastily assumed, though not by that critic himself, that such passages are alone historically trustworthy. This is an entirely unwarrantable conclusion; but the fact that these passages, which may be considered as at least awkward, are recorded shows that we are dealing with historical facts and not with mere invention, and the honesty of the writers in retaining such sayings provides us with a general guarantee of their honesty throughout.

Another argument for the credibility of the Gospels may be drawn from the distinction between the recorded words and the described works of Jesus. The descriptions are, of course, the Evangelist's own, and it is here, if anywhere, that we might expect exaggeration, for at any rate, it is here that the Evangelist would feel free to record events not only as they impressed him, but in order to convey an adequate impression to others. But it is less likely that the words of Jesus would be altered; moreover, they have a characteristic style which it is difficult to

THE CREDIBILITY OF THE GOSPELS

imitate, and would be betraying to change or adapt. But in addition to the wonderful sobriety and purely objective narrative to which the Evangelists limit themselves, the words of Jesus constantly contain indirect evidence of the truth of the Evangelists' record. In answer to the inquiries of the Baptist's disciples, Jesus declares that "the blind receive their sight, and the lame walk, and the lepers are cleansed, and the deaf hear, and the dead are raised up." Recorded words of Jesus similarly refer to the miraculous feeding both of the five thousand and the four thousand, which many critics have taken to be a double account of the same event. We cannot prove in any particular instance that the words of Jesus have not been carefully adapted to the record, but we can argue that this was not a general practice from the fact that Christ's word "no sign shall be given to this generation" is allowed to stand; which indeed some critics have quoted as a proof that Jesus never wrought any miracles at all. His frequent prediction that He would rise again " after three days " is left unaltered, despite the fact that all the Gospels record that He rose after a shorter period. None of these difficulties may be beyond explanation, but the Evangelists leave the difficulties standing without any attempt to explain them away.

Again, radical criticism at one time was willing to cut out from the Gospels the whole miraculous element, even though this would leave the Gospels consisting chiefly of lacunæ, entailing the deletion of many of Christ's words as well as whole masses of the Evangelists' descriptions. But just because modern psycho-therapeutics can perform what are taken to be at least approximations to some of Christ's healing works, many of His miracles are now admitted to be credible; of course, largely because it is believed that they were not miracles at all. But if it is now admitted that events thought to be incredible are now believed to have been possible, by what process of criticism can we still cut out works which go beyond anything that modern science has discovered to be possible? To the Evangelists all Christ's works were wrought by the same power, and the fact that we now think some of these likely to be true records of what happened surely carries with it the presumption that records of others are likely to be true also; they did not know the difference between what we regard as possible and impossible to faith healing, and they record what are to us the more incredible things in the same calm style and with the same circumstantial detail.

Finally, all criticism has drawn attention to the remarkable difference between the first three Gospels and the Fourth, a difference which no one can overlook, and which extends not only to the order and the material, but to the style of diction and the content of the message. And this is so diverse, that it is felt by many that the Synoptics and the Fourth Gospel cannot both be historical: we must choose between them. But even radical critics have not been averse from using the Fourth Gospel to show that sometimes the Synoptics may be wrong; for instance, in the coincidence of the Passover with the Last Supper, and the length of time Jesus was actually on the cross. It has also been pointed out that the Synoptic framework encloses a mere fragment of Christ's ministry, and here and there it shows signs that there are really gaps in what at first looks like a continuous narrative; so that although the Synoptics seem to confine Christ's ministry to Galilee, with only one short visit to Jerusalem, and that at the end of

His life, the record in the Fourth Gospel of a Judæan ministry, interspersed by visits to Galilee, is not chronologically inconceivable. It must be admitted, however, that the Fourth Gospel is engaged with open controversy between Christ and the Jews concerning His authority and personality, while such discussions are absent from the Synoptics. Nevertheless we do find links that form a sort of bridge between the two. The Fourth Gospel contains not only echoes, but reproductions of the Synoptic teaching: for instance, " he that loveth his life shall lose it, and he that hateth his life in this world shall keep it unto life eternal " ; while the passage in the Synoptics in which Jesus claims that all things have been committed to Him, and that the Son alone knows the Father, is in the same style and of the same concern as much of the teaching in the Fourth Gospel ; so also is the question raised by Jesus in the Synoptics as to how the Christ can be David's Lord and yet his son. Moreover, it is interesting to note that on the great issue of Christ's claim to divinity, precisely where the diversity between the Synoptics and the Fourth Gospel is felt to be most critical, there is exactly the same reticence in both: neither in the Synoptics nor in the Fourth Gospel does Jesus ever claim in so many words to be God ; in both it is left to be inferred from what He does claim, and the highest point to which the personality of Christ is raised is in both not His own claim, but a confession, in the one, made by St. Peter and, in the other, by St. Thomas. There is no doubt that the author of the Fourth Gospel was writing under the conviction that Jesus was the Logos, and that this is his explanation of His personality ; but never does he put this explanation forward as one which Jesus Himself made. It is true that the style in which the Fourth

Gospel is written is so uniform that sometimes we cannot tell whether the words are to be taken as the Evangelist's own comment or the record of what Jesus said; and from a comparison with the style of the Epistle ascribed to the same author we are forced to conclude that it is the Evangelist's own. Can we feel the same confidence therefore that in this Gospel we have a true record of what Jesus said? It can be seen that we cannot answer this in a dogmatically negative fashion unless we are willing to face the conclusion that this Evangelist is simply reading his own thoughts into the mind of Jesus. But if we compare the quality of his thought in his own Epistle with chapters xiv to xvii of the Gospel, to think that these latter were simply invented by a disciple of Jesus, however intimate, involves the psychological contradiction that he was a man who had little concern for the truth, and yet possessed a mind whose insight into spiritual truth must be ranked above the mind of Jesus Himself. If we may take it for granted that the Fourth Gospel was written by an intimate disciple many years after the other Gospels had been written, with the desire not to traverse the same ground, entirely in his own style (which, it must be remembered, is simply a question of literal or free translation), and in order to bring out the more intimate teaching of Jesus as it threw light upon the questions which had come to be raised concerning His personality; and if, on the other hand, we can assume that the Synoptic Gospels contain a selection from the teaching of Jesus specially designed only as an introduction to the Christian Faith, then we seem if not to be in possession of a detailed and entirely complete reconciliation, yet to have good ground for believing that such a reconciliation existed in the actual, historical facts.

THE CREDIBILITY OF THE GOSPELS

It seems possible to detect other reasons for a selective process which help to account for the differences between the Synoptics themselves, and still more for the difference between the Synoptics and St. John. Criticism seems to have established that the Gospel according to St. Mark was the earliest complete outline, and the tradition is that this was written as the reminiscences of St. Peter's own preaching. At the same time it is held, though with less certainty, that there existed a collection of the sayings of Jesus, which may have been written originally by St. Matthew, and this seems to have been mainly for the purpose of instructing people in the ethical side of the Christian religion. When St. Matthew's and St. Luke's Gospels came to be written it was the authority of St. Peter that led both of them to take the framework of St. Mark's Gospel, throughout which the collection of the " Sayings " was differently distributed. But if we may believe that the writer of the Fourth Gospel was also an intimate disciple (which is, of course, openly claimed); and if we can go further and assume that the beloved disciple was the Apostle John (as is also indirectly claimed, since he is otherwise never mentioned in this Gospel by name); and also that he wrote his Gospel in extreme old age in Ephesus (and such is the tradition which was handed down in direct line through Irenæus and Polycarp, the latter an immediate disciple of St. John); then we may account for the differences between the Gospels in such a way as to make them all in a sufficient measure trustworthy.

The conclusion of the whole matter, therefore, is that the most thoroughgoing legitimate criticism does not reveal any conceivable process by which the Gospels have been gradually evolved by a process of exaggeration, legendary accretion and theological adaptation from something that in its original was not even capable of becoming a gospel; and the very ruthlessness of radical criticism has laid bare a foundation of historic credibility on which we may safely build the assurance of the credibility of the Gospels as a whole. This does not involve that there are no signs in the Gospels of adaptation to accord with prophecy, of a heightening of the wonder of the narrative, or of the elimination of material on reverential grounds; but this is all exceedingly slight, and what can be detected rather increases than destroys the evidence for the veracity of the narrative as a whole. It does not deny that we have widely differing portraits in the Synoptics and in the Fourth Gospel; but while the former are content with something more corresponding to a photograph and a phonographic record, the latter is a portrait painted by a master hand and a record which a master mind has told in his own language so as to portray and bring out the spiritual intention and the eternal significance of Christ's words. And if these two pictures are taken as complementary, we may have every confidence that the Gospels bring us in contact with historic events and the mind of an actual personality of such a fashion that we can be sure that this life has a critical meaning for all human history, and that this personality cannot be accounted for save as the Incarnation of God.

IV

THE TEACHING OF JESUS

WHATEVER controversy may have arisen and still exists about Jesus Christ, the derivation, explanation and significance of His person, all are agreed that He was a great religious teacher, one of the greatest the world has known, if not the greatest of all. Although the actual quantity of His teaching which has been preserved is slight, for the actual words of Christ in the Gospels can be read by anybody in two hours, yet even this quantity is considerable when compared with what we possess of other early religious teachers who have any claim to be regarded as original. But what gives Christ His claim to greatness as a teacher is the extraordinary pregnancy of His teaching; there is so much content in so little that it has proved an inexhaustible source of wisdom to those who have studied it, its provocative challenge only increases with the growth of knowledge, and its beauty exercises an unfading attraction to the weary hearts of men. It is due to no accident or advantage, but solely to its indisputable merits, that the teaching of Jesus has called forth a greater body of comment, explanation and controversy than the words of anyone else; and so far from diminishing, this only increases, and after two thousand years of civilization and culture is a sufficient testimony to its permanent interest and vital importance.

The teaching of Jesus has not only been studied for its great ethical and religious value, it has

THE TEACHING OF JESUS

been closely scanned in order that we may arrive at a clear conception of Christ's nature and mission and, if possible, answer the questions which have been raised about Him, who He was and what He means for our race. But it is precisely the use of the teaching of Christ as a court of appeal for the solution of these problems which has in modern times led only to the deepening of the problems and the emergence of endless controversy. It has been claimed that if we confine ourselves to the teaching of Jesus it completely disposes of the idea that He regarded Himself as anything extraordinary, as a worker of wonders, a revealer of supernatural truth or as a person uniquely related to God; so that the whole structure of ecclesiastical doctrine concerning Christ is rejected by many as a complete misunderstanding of, and departure from, His teaching. And sometimes this reading of the situation is held to be confirmed by the alleged fact that the people who believe in the Godhead of Jesus take little notice of His teaching, while the people who believe that His teaching ought to be followed generally do not believe in His Godhead. When, however, this position is faced with the general outlook of the teaching contained in the Fourth Gospel, or by certain sayings contained in the Synoptics, these are dismissed as out of accord with the general outlook and undisputed sayings of the Synoptics, and are regarded as a product of the early misunderstanding of Jesus, rather than the words of Jesus Himself. But this hasty dismissal of elements out of harmony with a theory is more and more coming to be recognized as due rather to preconceived notions and impatient dislike of certain ideas than to any valid principles or legitimate application of literary criticism.

It needs to be pointed out that this concentration of attention on the teaching of Jesus is itself unbalanced: beside the teaching of Jesus there went His ministry of healing, and the people who thronged around Him were impressed equally by both. What astonished people about Christ's teaching was firstly its authority and secondly its grace. He did not appeal to authority, but He spoke as if He possessed it. He spoke as one who knew, and that not merely with dogmatic asseveration, for His words were peculiarly gracious. This means that His hearers were conscious of a singular freedom from mere strenuousness of utterance, as if Jesus had to labour to produce conviction. The very ease with which everything was said and the beauty with which it was clothed showed how spontaneously it sprang from His soul. And it had the effect of conveying grace to the hearers; that is, it secured the assent of the mind, touched the emotions and swayed the will. It was unique teaching, not merely didactic and informative, but conveying and creative. Moreover, Christ's public ministry occupied only about one-tenth of His life, and although that life was violently cut short and His teaching began at what was, for the custom of the time, a somewhat early age, yet the silent years of His manhood bear a proportion to His public ministry whose significance cannot be overlooked. Again, of the actual period occupied by His ministry, the teaching of which we have a record could have occupied only the merest fraction of that time. It only confirms the obvious conclusion of these considerations that Christ's teaching was apparently so haphazard. He Himself wrote not a line, nor do we possess any statement which shows that He commissioned others to record His teaching; there is a comparative lack of anything like systematic instruction; much of the teaching is not in the form of deliberate and spontaneous utterance, but is only called forth by some event or by an actual question; while often it is imparted in such private conversations that it is a problem as to how it ever got recorded at all. Some of Christ's most important teaching must depend upon the report of a single person, and that not always a person who would be regarded as most fitted to record the conversation. Not only so, but Jesus was at no pains to make Himself understood; whenever His teaching was complained of as being difficult, the added explanation does little to remove the difficulty, but seems rather deliberately intended to maintain, if not to increase it. A considerable part of the teaching was conveyed by means of parables, and the difficulty of their interpretation is carried to the point of perplexity when it is explained that the parabolic form was chosen not in order to make the truth simple and easily remembered, but that it might be more effectively concealed. It is obvious, therefore, that Jesus could not have regarded His teaching as we regard it. The Gospels as we know them were clearly written not primarily to preserve Christ's teaching, but to tell us the good news of how the Son of God came into the world, how He lived, and still more how He died.

Christ's apparent carelessness about His teaching, His comparative unconcern to make Himself understood, and the haphazard method He followed, are nevertheless no proof that He did not regard His message as highly important and was not anxious to impart it to men. But His manner and method of teaching were dictated by His clear understanding of what true teaching must always be. He knew that truth cannot be conveyed to men merely by a clear statement made by somebody else; He wanted them to search for it and discover it for themselves. Moreover, as a teacher possessing His insight He must have known that men learn more from example than from exhortation, and His teaching, by the very perfection which it commands, is meant to help men to the discovery that they cannot rise to such heights unless they have not only embraced a new principle of life, but have received a new power of carrying it into effect. And therefore always behind the teaching stands the personality of the teacher, and what He seeks to convey is something more than information; it is spirit and life. How Jesus conceived His teaching was to become operative in men's life we shall have to consider later.

If these considerations are borne in mind and given due weight to, we can, however, go on to maintain that the teaching, if a secondary element in the life of Christ, is of immense importance and is bound to be the final court of appeal. The famous statement of Dr. Dale's that " Christ did not come so much to preach a Gospel as that there should be a Gospel to preach," while a necessary correction to a widely current misunderstanding, is nevertheless only a paradox, and if pressed too far would entail our regarding a great deal of Christ's activity as not only wasted, but mistaken. It will be found that we need have no fears that a careful and impartial consideration of Christ's teaching will do anything but confirm the Gospel story in which it has been set, and the great structure of Christian faith which has been erected upon it. It is too late in the day to try to reverse the process by which Christ's teaching has developed into what we know as Christianity. We hold that it was both a natural and a divinely guided process. The discrediting of Christianity would discredit the teaching of Christ, which certainly contains the elements on which Christianity is built, and if He had not foreseen these developments, and either taken steps to prevent them or intended to sanction them, He would have been lacking in prudence or understanding; in short, a most unwise and uninstructed teacher. The attempts made to play off the teaching of Christ against Christianity have all proved themselves too arbitrary, hasty and uncritical to warrant any further attention being given to them. They have had a century of patient consideration; it is time they were recognized as having missed the mark.

When, however, we set ourselves to gather a general impression of what Jesus taught, we find ourselves confronted with a well-nigh impossible task, for there is nothing more difficult than to try to systematize, summarize or expound the teaching of Jesus; for His teaching does not consist so much in the enunciation of abstract principles as in the application of truth to concrete cases. Jesus prefers the method of paradox, hyperbole and vivid illustration, so that His sayings often appear to be exaggerations or inconsistent with other sayings that can be set against them. He will embody some great principle in an exhortation to unconventional action; and then the literalists fail to grasp the principle and the allegorists to act upon it. Truth is either conveyed by means of parables, where a story is worked out in considerable detail, but where nevertheless the lesson intended is often of a single and simple character, or it is compressed into sayings so terse that they seem tied up past all unravelling, and the most discursive exposition of them fails to set forth the meaning half as well as the pregnant, aphoristic original. There are occasional longer discourses, such as the Sermon on the Mount, or the eschatological teaching given on the Temple Hill; but these have been suspected to be partially compilations, and in the case of the former the stream of paradox and closely packed sayings is about as unlike a sermon as anything we can conceive. To translate this teaching into other terms seems only to reduce it to an uninspiring statement of abstract principles and to destroy its pungency and beauty. And yet we are invited to the task by Christ's own grouping of His teaching around two great phrases, one, the " Kingdom of God," and the other, " the Son of man." Vast research on the meaning of these phrases has been undertaken, but with inconclusive results. The second of these phrases we must leave until we come to examine the consciousness of Christ, and we can only note here that the questions scholars have raised but have left undecided are : whether the Kingdom of God is an inner experience or a visible social order ; whether it is present or future ; and whether it belongs to this world or to the world to come. There is no room here for a detailed discussion, but the simplest solution seems to be that the Kingdom of God is all these things. It is an inner surrender to the sovereign rule of God, and the more deeply and widely that surrender is made, the more this will translate itself into visible expression, and so make profound changes in the social, political and economic order. The Kingdom of God is also meant to be a state of society, realized in this world ; but its full realization can never be solely in an outward order or its complete fulfilment only in this life. The interior realization will always be in advance of the exterior, and the life of the world to come will always be needed to complete, and even to inspire, the conception of the Kingdom of God on earth.

But a phrase like the " Kingdom of God " is only as it were a container, and a centre of reference for Christ's teaching ; and we shall discover its meaning not so much by a linguistic examination of the phrase, or by tracing it to its origin, as by examining the teaching which alone expounds its content. Therefore it will probably be found more helpful, and we may retain something of the original inspiration and pointed application of His teaching if we set ourselves to inquire what Christ taught about certain things—for instance, about life, man, God, religion, sin; not attempting the impossible and unfruitful task of merely collecting together the sayings which could be arranged under these varied headings, nor, on the other hand, attempting the inevitable subjective and highly disputable task of reducing everything to formal principles, but simply endeavouring to bring out the point and maintain the balance of Christ's teaching.

What Christ has fundamentally to say about *life* is that as lived by most its importance is mistaken. Men live this life as if they were going to live here for ever; they imagine that its security and its joy consist in things, in having an abundance of things and in possessing them absolutely for their own. They are constantly heaping up treasures which are exposed to decay and despoiling; in short, man is a worldling, and hence his anxieties, his misunderstandings, his enmities. But on the other hand Jesus does not teach unworldliness in the sense that man is not to care about this life at all : this life is important down to every detail and to every word we speak. Its importance must be judged in the light of the world to come, which indeed makes this life not of less importance, but of enormously increased importance; we are so to use our possessions that we shall accumulate spiritual treasures and establish relationships with others that death cannot break. If we seek the perfect justice of the Kingdom of God, it will actually make a difference to the sufficiency and the security of our common necessities, will lessen our anxieties and increase the beauty of earthly conditions. To live this life in the light of eternity is Christ's remedy for putting this life right, and it is a sufficient commentary on how far we have missed His meaning that other-worldliness and this-worldliness have in turn brought this life to such disorder and misery. Christ believed that love for other persons was a constant entanglement, and that we must be prepared, if necessary, to put all human relationships on one side for the love of God. And yet He taught that to excuse our duty to our parents on some pretence of religion, or to seek release from marriage vows on any pretext, was wrong. He means, of course, that if we only love God first and with sufficient purity, we shall love all others rightly, to their benefit and our own; and not less, but much more, than if we had love them first and only.

Christ's teaching about *man* is as diverse as man's own almost infinitely varied, mixed and changeable nature. His parables show that He is under no delusions about mankind in general; there are few good persons in His parables; they are mostly cunning, boorish or small-minded, and if they do anything good it is often from a wrong motive. Christ knew that the heart of man was the great manufactory of most of the miseries which afflict life, and yet He held the greatest hope about man, exhorting him to behave with the indiscriminate generosity of God, bidding him to start ideal action towards others without waiting for them, not changing his tactics or losing hope if it elicited no response. He demanded, and believed man capable of, the sacrifice of home, comfort, reputation and life itself, if His service required it; He exhorted men to be perfect and with the perfection of God Himself. And all this obviously means that while Christ sees man as he is, He believes that man as he is is not what he ought to be or can be, and while the change from the one to the other involves going back, unlearning everything and starting all over again, He believes that this is possible if man will repent and have faith and seek the help of God.

Christ's teaching about *God* makes God extraordinarily familiar, caring for mankind not only in the mass, but as individuals; not that God simply cares for everyone alike, for a solitary soul wandering from Him would concern Him more than any number who were safe: God matches His care according to our need, the sinful exciting in Him not revulsion, but special solicitude. Yet Christ recognizes how many things there are in this life which seem to conflict with God's special care of the individual, but He brushes aside the idea that we can judge God's care by the external happenings and accidents of life: God cares for men more than for sparrows, and even though the sparrow sometimes falls out of the nest and is killed, that does not mean that God does not care. God cares for men to the very hairs of their head, and yet He may call them to go through pain and suffering, and so far from delivering them from destruction, may expect them to die a martyr's death. It must be, therefore, for the souls of men that God cares; but this can only be learned by an interior faith that trusts God's ultimate purpose and takes everything that happens as a means towards its realization. So, while Jesus teaches men to pray even for their daily bread, this prayer must be set within the ultimate purposes of God, and its complete answer is dependent on the one hand upon the coming of the Kingdom and on the other on men being forgiven and forgiving. The intimate familiarity with God to which the soul is introduced is never for a moment allowed to detract or diminish from the greatness and the holiness of God; and while Jesus often seems to base His argument for God's behaviour on imperfect human goodness, declaring that God must be much better than that, God's transcendence of all human standards is made regulative of all our thought concerning Him.

Christ's teaching about *religion* is distinctive and emphatic in its insistence upon the interior spiritual disposition, without which all external expression is not only useless, but a pretence and deceit. No kind of outward observance done to honour God can cover up, or be a substitute for the neglect of common duty. And yet with all this insistence upon interior sincerity and our duty towards men, Jesus never speaks against external observance as such or makes human duty a sufficient substitute for the worship of God. Even when He criticizes the Pharisees for paying such attention to the minutiæ of ritual while they neglected the greater matters of the Law, Jesus did not propose they should merely reverse their concern, but that they should give the right place to both. Even if a man ought to seek reconciliation with his brother before he brings an offering to God, Jesus recognized that it was the making of the offering that tends to bring our duty to our brother to mind, and when we have discharged that duty, we must return to offer our gift. The love of our neighbour must be inspired by loving God with the total capacity of our whole nature, and measured by our love for ourselves. This may be altruism, but it is in an unusual setting of religion and reason. Naturally Christ's teaching has a good deal to say about prayer, which is the very heart of religion, and Jesus undoubtedly gives to prayer a positively stupendous power, sanctioning petition both for the simplest necessities and the most miraculous happenings, but that prayer must be placed within the scheme of God's perfect will for all men, and it must be interpreted by a faith which not only believes that all things are possible, but trusts God sufficiently to know that all prayer is rightly answered, even when it seems not to be. The fact that God must know what we need before we ask is for Jesus no argument or excuse against prayer, but the very ground of its working, and the assurance that if it is really our need it will be granted.

Jesus does not appear to teach very much concerning *sin*, if we are looking for some analysis or description of what sin is. He seems to be more concerned with assuring people that sin can be forgiven; but while his judgments on sin are sufficiently grave He reverses the comparative gravity with which different types of sin are regarded even by religious people. His comparison of the religious prospects of the Scribes and Pharisees on the one hand, and the harlots and publicans on the other, shows that sins due to the temptations of the flesh and the world are not necessarily so grave in their effect upon the soul as sins due to complacency and self-righteousness. On the other hand, Jesus never takes lenient views about sin; He regards man as creating sin out of his own heart, and this is the origin of the lawlessness and misery which afflict mankind; and rather than sin through the temptation of eye or hand, He counsels the most drastic asceticism, because of the remorse and pain that all sin is bound to bring. Men should suffer anything rather than sin; it is the sinner, not the sufferer, who is to be pitied. There is a sin which He regards as unpardonable in this world or the next, but so far from this being some peculiar form of sin that very few are likely to fall into, it is the sin to which all sin, if persisted in, at last must lead, the perversion of good into evil, so that the judgment of right and wrong is reversed and repentance is impossible. Jesus says very little about how the forgiveness of sins is actually wrought, either in the will of God or in its effect upon man; but while the Father is always ready to forgive, forgiveness is not a mere enunciation of pardon, for it is ineffective until it has begotten in man a forgiving spirit in turn; and Jesus spoke of the necessity of His giving His life in order to ransom man from the delusion and bondage of sin, and looked to the shedding of His blood as necessary for its remission.

It can be seen from this rough summary of what Jesus taught upon these important questions in what sense His teaching can be called original and complete. It accepts the main ideas to which the prophetic revelation had reached as true, and adds very little that cannot be paralleled from the Old Testament. The originality of Christ's teaching is to be sought rather in the insight into the interior dispositions which theological notions demand and the unconventional applications of accepted moral principles. He does not alter accepted ideas so much as show how revolutionary they are, if sincerely accepted and seriously followed. It is this freshness of treatment and these pointed references which give life to His teaching and have made it a perpetual challenge to the consciousness and conduct of men.

Jesus would have been strangely lacking in moral insight, and could hardly be counted a great teacher at all, if He had not realized that man is an adept at coining moral maxims, and that human wisdom already abounded with moral exhortations. He must have known that man was in need of superior power and supernatural grace if he was ever to live up even to his own ideals. So Christ expressed His ethical teaching in extreme and exigent form in order to break down man's complacency, and to show him how far he fell short, and how impossible was any true attainment without great inward change. Do the Gospels show how this change is to be wrought? There is no doubt that the Fourth Gospel is taken up with meeting this very point, and without that Gospel the teaching in the Synoptics would remain mostly only a challenge to attempt the impossible. The difference between the Synoptics and the Fourth Gospel has been previously admitted, some explanation of that difference given and a reconciliation attempted: the present issue involves a further confirmation of that previously established position; for the difference between the teaching of the Synoptics and the Fourth Gospel on this point can be roughly described as, on the one hand, ethical and, on the other, religious; or again as based on exhortation and example respectively. And this must be due in both cases to selection for a specific purpose. But there is sufficient of the ethical emphasis in the Fourth Gospel and of religious emphasis in the Synoptics to bridge over the difference between the two. In the Synoptics Jesus complains of those who call Him Lord and do not the things that He says; in the Fourth Gospel He teaches that if men love Him they will keep His commandments: a faith dictated by personal love is the motive of obedience. In the Synoptics, when Jesus inculcates upon the young man seeking eternal life the keeping of the Commandments, it is to be noted that He enumerates only those of the second Table of the Decalogue, and that when He goes on to counsel perfection, this consists not only in renunciation of possessions and the taking up of the cross, but also the following of Him; and this obviously takes the place of the first Table of the Decalogue. In essence this only sets forth the reiterated message of the Fourth

Gospel, that eternal life can be attained only by an interior assimilation of Christ, and a constant abiding in a deep personal love for Him. In the Fourth Gospel Jesus sets Himself forth as the ultimate principle of eternal Life which He is able to impart to those who believe on Him; and this means nothing less than the complete surrender of the will to Christ and the making of Him the central and governing power of one's being. But this is only a religious and psychological explanation of what is demanded in the Synoptics when Jesus calls upon men to lose their life for His sake and the Gospel's. The attempt, therefore, to make a distinction between Christ's ethical and religious teaching is false and impossible; they are woven together inseparably, and the person who can praise the ethical teaching of Jesus and not see the need for Christ's example which, it must be remembered, ended in the Cross, and in that example more than a mere encouragement, but one which is actually able to convey the necessary power, is surely convicted of taking Christ's ethical teaching in a most superficial way. That teaching calls us to nothing less than the living of this life as the sons of God, that is behaving in our human conditions according to the mind and will and ways of God. We need someone to teach us what these are, and no one can so teach us or lift us to that divine height save God Himself. The person who declares to us the divine will as Christ has done, must be Himself divine if His teaching is to have any authority; but still more so must the person be none other than God if He is to convey moral power to enable us to reach the height of divine perfection; for this can only be done by the elevation of the human heart to a love and a worship which God alone can inspire, and by an interior union with, and transformation of, the human spirit of which God alone is capable. And therefore the teaching of Jesus can only be understood when the exhortation of the Synoptics is combined with the method of religious regeneration taught in the Fourth Gospel; the authority which it manifests only explained by assuming a divine consciousness from which it arises; and its power only realized as we take into account the example of a sinless life, which ended in a death that is a revelation of sin, the seal of its forgiveness, and the means of taking sin away.

V

THE CONSCIOUSNESS OF CHRIST

THE consciousness of Christ is a somewhat ambiguous, but sufficiently wide phrase under which may conveniently be grouped a number of related questions of immense importance for our understanding of the personality of Jesus Christ. But the phrase is specially selected at this point to enable us to make a psychological rather than a dogmatic approach to the problem of Christ's personality. We are here concerned not so much with what others thought of Jesus, but with what He thought of Himself; and the term "consciousness" may be used to indicate that of which His mind was immediately aware, rather than His formulated thought or utterances based upon that awareness. Modern criticism compels us to make a distinction between what others thought Jesus to be, and what He thought Himself to be; and psychological criticism compels us to distinguish between an immediate awareness and a reasoned conviction. Once these distinctions have been raised in connection with the personality of Jesus, we must consider the problems they present; and to inquire not only whether there is a difference between what others thought of Christ and what He thought of Himself, but also whether any distinction can be drawn between the immediate consciousness of Jesus and His own statements about Himself. We must remember at every point in the discussion how much we are dependent, first of all,

THE CONSCIOUSNESS OF CHRIST

upon the Evangelists for their record of Christ's self-disclosure, and secondly upon Himself, for we can only know what He has disclosed. But since modern analytical psychology believes it is able to penetrate beyond a person's statements to the state of his consciousness, and even to penetrate deeper to a realm of his mind of which the person may be entirely unconscious, and since this method is likely to be applied more and more to the problem of Christ's personality, we must be willing to follow that method so far as it is possible and to consider any conclusions it demands. Although such a method is full of pitfalls, and often gives rise to dogmatic conclusions based on imperfect and indecisive evidence, it must be admitted that the problem of Christ's personality peculiarly invites this method; for Christ often prefers to learn what others think of Him rather than to impose His own convictions upon them, so that there is a studied reticence about His self-disclosure which compels us to explore His consciousness by indirect means. With this wide understanding of the meaning of the phrase " the consciousness of Christ," and with the object of penetrating as far as we can, and by every route available, into the mind of Jesus, we may set ourselves to explore both what His direct statements declare and His indirect disclosures involve.

It seems necessary to assume that Jesus had an immediate consciousness of God. The human mind comes to a consciousness of God through a process which often takes considerable time to work out, which is due to the confluence of a number of conclusions and is based upon accumulated experiences of various kinds. This process is bound to impart a particular character to our belief, and hence in all human thought about God a considerable space is devoted to argument. This is conspicuously and significantly absent in Jesus. There is another type of God-consciousness with which the Old Testament Scriptures have made us familiar, namely, the prophetic; here also there is a great absence of argument about God's character or proof of His action. The Old Testament prophet constantly prefaces his utterances by the formula, "Thus saith the Lord," and then speaks as if God were speaking through him; and often with accompanying psychic manifestations, as if he were speaking in a trance, as one possessed, or under profound inspiration, his own normal personality seeming to be in abeyance or abnormally exalted. Now Jesus never uses the prophetic formula; although He is hailed as a prophet and refers to His experiences as those which a prophet can only expect, yet He declared that the prophetic succession came to an end with John the Baptist, and when He receives the report that others regard Him as one of the prophets, He presses His disciples to confess whether they regard Him as anything more. When making statements which involve taking upon Himself supreme authority or requiring solemn affirmation, He does not say, "Thus saith the Lord," but is content to say, "I say unto you," or, as constantly in the Johannine record, "Verily, verily I say unto you." Again, the mystical consciousness has made us familiar with its peculiar certainty about God; though this certainty that God is, and is near to the soul, is generally balanced by an unwillingness to say what God is, or how He is known to be near to the soul, which indeed is constantly affirmed to be indescribable. But neither is Christ's consciousness of God like this mystical consciousness; it has the same certainty, but never employs its fervent affirmation, which sufficiently indicates that

THE CONSCIOUSNESS OF CHRIST

it is of recent growth and can be compared with a previous lack of certainty. Christ's consciousness of God therefore seems to be different from the rational, the prophetic and the mystical type : it may embrace them all, but in doing so it completely transcends them. Christ speaks about God with such a calm certainty, that it seems as natural, indubitable and immediate to Him as our consciousness of the external world. In one most important passage, found both in St. Matthew and St. Luke, He declares that He knows the Father as no one else knows or can know Him ; and that mankind is dependent upon Himself, the Son, if it is to arrive at a similar knowledge. The historicity of this statement is on literary grounds beyond suspicion, but just because it is a direct statement and a dogmatic affirmation, the critical mind is suspicious of it. It should be noted that the whole passage is expressed in the third person, " No one knoweth the Son, save the Father," and although this is perhaps an indication that it springs from an immediate consciousness, we should not demand that great emphasis be placed upon it unless it were supported by other evidence of immediacy, which, however, we have seen to be available. Christ's consciousness of God is therefore of such a character as inevitably to raise the question who He Himself can be, for His consciousness of God demands something more than a *special revelation*, which would naturally express itself after the prophetic type ; it demands a *special relation* to God.

The next question which therefore falls to be explored is in what sense Jesus conceived Himself to be the Messiah. This question raises a whole series of problems, but the important ones for our purpose are, firstly, how far Jesus, according to the Gospels, accepted the title of the Messiah, and

THE CONSCIOUSNESS OF CHRIST

secondly, whether in the Old Testament the idea of the Messiah had ever advanced beyond the position of an agent of God. Both these problems are involved in the significance underlying the ascription to Jesus of the title " Son of God." As far as the Gospels are concerned, it must be noted that this title is ascribed to Jesus, first, by the devil hypothetically, then by the demon-possessed; it is this which St. Peter confesses, and finally, at the trial before Caiaphas, Jesus is adjured to declare whether He is the Son of God. Does the Son of God in all these cases mean only the Messiah ? The two terms are frequently found side by side in the Gospels, "Christ, the Son of God "; is the second only the explanation of the first ? Comparing together the way in which the Messianic king in the Old Testament is called " my Son," and the way in which Caiaphas declared that Christ was guilty of blasphemy in assenting to his question, we are driven to conclude that " Son of God " is assuming something more than the relationship of a mere agent. In the Fourth Gospel the use of the term " Son of God " obviously carries the higher meaning. It is interesting, therefore, if somewhat perplexing, to notice that this title is, in the Synoptics, not claimed, but only accepted by Jesus from others, and then with an apparent element of dislike or discontent. Was this because of its Messianic significance, or because it seemed to Him to go too far, and savour of divinity ? There can be no hesitation that it was the Messianic significance with which He was discontented, for we find He takes a similar attitude towards the straightforward title for the Messiah, " the Christ." On one occasion Jesus asks the Pharisees " What think ye of Christ, whose son is he ? " And then quoting the 110th Psalm He asks, " If David then called him Lord, how is he his son?" Now there is no longer any disagreement amongst scholars that Christ did regard Himself as the promised Messiah. He is not therefore in this discussion with the Pharisees repudiating the idea that He is the Messiah and therefore David's son, but he is pointing out that the Christ cannot be merely David's son, since David calls him Lord. All this seems to imply therefore that Jesus regarded Himself as the Son of God in a real and not merely titular sense. Yet we are faced with the fact that the Son of God was not the title He preferred, but the title " Son of man."

The meaning of the phrase " the Son of man " has led to voluminous research without, however, many certain conclusions being reached. If we could be sure that Christ was adopting this title from the apocalyptic Book of Enoch, two things would be certain: firstly, that it was a Messianic title, and, secondly, that it was not therefore chosen as a means of humbly protesting that He was a mere man. But if this title was already well known to be a name for the Messiah, then its adoption would have defeated Christ's obvious purpose of concealing from the multitude that He was the Messiah. The Book of Enoch may not have been widely known at that time, and it is even possible that the verses in which " the Son of man " occurs in that Book are later interpolations; in that case we should be driven to look to the Book of Daniel for the origin of the phrase, where obviously it denotes a being in close relation to " the Ancient of Days." But if we examine Christ's actual use of the phrase we shall gain more light. It seems to be used by Him in two sets of contrasted sayings: firstly, those which refer to His power to forgive sins and to legislate for the Sabbath, which is in strange contrast to the saying where the Son of man is declared to have nowhere to lay His head; and, secondly, those which speak of His coming again "in glory," with which are contrasted those that declare that suffering and death must come first. Now, although this seems to confront us with a perfect maze of ambiguity, it can be put forward with some confidence that the following explanation is a clue to Christ's adoption of the term.

The constant reiteration of the phrase is meant to conceal His claims from the careless, for His constant speaking of Himself in the third person would hide from many that He was referring to Himself at all, while it would awaken inquiry in the earnest, as in the Fourth Gospel it is actually reported to have done: "Who is this Son of man?" This is all in accordance with Christ's general method of teaching. His emphasis upon being the Son of man, while drawing attention to His humanity, by that very fact would emphasise that He was more than human, or human only by His own choice and for some great purpose. There is no need for the ordinary human being to go about this world declaring that he is human; there was a necessity for Christ to do that; and when this is done to draw attention to His lowly condition, and yet to the power He inherently possessed; to the fact that He must suffer an ignominious death, and yet that He was coming again in glory, it seems to point to the only possible conclusion, that He is a glorious being who has *become man*. If it can be pressed that in the Book of Daniel "the Son of man" is a personal symbol for the kingdom of the saints, even this can be read into Christ's use of the term, for as the Son of God He had become Son of man in order to teach the sons of men how to become the sons of God. It is confirmatory of this conclusion to notice that Jesus refers to the

THE CONSCIOUSNESS OF CHRIST

experience of suffering which the Son of man must undergo as if that had been predicted; but there is no such prediction discoverable. That can be found, however, attached to the idea of "the Servant of the Lord," spoken of so frequently in the second half of the Book of Isaiah. It seems clear that Jesus has adopted the *idea* of the "suffering servant" under the *name* of the "Son of man." Apparently He did not care to describe Himself as the Servant of the Lord; He was His Son, not a servant.

Is it possible to move with any confidence beyond this realm of somewhat ambiguous terminology and to ask what it implies for the immediate self-consciousness of Christ? Now, although it seems an unpromising start, where we have so much of our basic evidence doubtful or in dispute, if we only remember that this ambiguity was intentional on Christ's part, then we may find ourselves in possession of a solution to many difficulties. It is clear enough from the Gospels that Jesus did desire His Messiahship to be concealed from the multitude, and this was obviously because it had come to wear a political significance which He could not accept, and its open adoption would only rouse expectations which He was bound to disappoint. At the same time, Jesus could not at the last deny His belief that He was the Messiah, for that would have conveyed a false impression: for He regarded Himself as the true and only fulfilment of the Messianic prophecies of the Old Testament. Yet Jesus was not contented with a purely Messianic rôle; His consciousness of unique relationship to God could not be expressed in terms suitable to a mere agent, or commissioned representative, however exalted. Nevertheless His discontent with official phraseology did not leave Him unable to describe the relationship to God of which He was

THE CONSCIOUSNESS OF CHRIST

immediately conscious. He occasionally uses a phrase, which is indubitably His own: it is that of "the Son," and the meaning this had for Him can be gathered from His constant use of the word "Father" as His name for God.

We have now to ask the question whether, when Jesus called Himself the Son, He was claiming for Himself anything more than what was common or possible to humanity. Does it fully describe His mission to say that He came to reveal that God was the Father of all men and all men were the sons of God, of which He Himself was only exemplar and norm? That the answer should be in dispute amongst students of the New Testament is not really due to the ambiguity of the evidence, but to the difficulty of stating the whole truth without doing injustice to some essential element in it. It would not be true to say that Jesus regarded Himself as the only Son of God, or to deny that He distinguished His Sonship from that of which others were capable. It seems to involve drafts upon later developed doctrine to say that Jesus regarded His Sonship as unique, and yet that He came to lift mankind to His own Sonship in dependence upon His revelation and in communion with His personality: but that is precisely what the Gospels necessitate and support. He is the Son who alone knows the Father, and who alone can reveal Him to others. But men can know the Father and they can become His sons. Nevertheless, Jesus always distinguishes His Sonship from that of others. The fact that Jesus never once placed Himself alongside His disciples by referring to God as "our Father," but always distinguishes "my Father" and "your heavenly Father," is significant, especially as this is obviously an undesigned negative agreement. The Lord's Prayer with its "Our Father" is no exception, for it

THE CONSCIOUSNESS OF CHRIST

is more correctly described in the Disciples' Prayer; there is no indication that Jesus used it or prayed it with them: "When ye pray, say, Our Father." The Fourth Gospel, while much more explicit on this point, does not contradict or go beyond, but only confirms this position. When Jesus, according to that Gospel, is accused, because "being a man He made Himself God," He appealed to the Scriptures, where men are actually called gods, and argued thus: "If He called them gods unto whom the word of God came . . . say ye of Him whom the Father sanctified and sent into the world, Thou blasphemest; because I said I am the Son of God?" This does not argue that Jesus is only God in the sense that all men can be described as in some sense divine; the force of the argument is that if man can in any sense be called God, *how much more* then the Son of God!

It seems clear, therefore, that Jesus regarded Himself as uniquely related to God, and that He regarded His relationship as so intimate as to be mutual: for as only the Son knew the Father, so only the Father knew the Son. What was the basis of this knowledge? Are we to say that Jesus was immediately conscious of Himself as a divine person? New Testament scholars have found reason to doubt this because Christ never says in so many words "I am God"; not even in the Fourth Gospel. But such a declaration would have been misleading and confusing to His hearers, brought up as they were in the strictest monotheistic doctrine; it would seem to them like claiming that He was the same person as the Eternal Father; but if He declares that He is the Son of the Father, this surely amounts to a claim that He is divine as the Father is: the Son of God could not really belong to another order than that

THE CONSCIOUSNESS OF CHRIST

of God Himself. In the Fourth Gospel it is recorded that Jesus said that to see Him was to see the Father, and that He was one with the Father. These are statements which cannot be paralleled in the Synoptics, and yet what else could His calling Himself the Son actually imply? It seems impossible to take this Sonship in a merely ethical sense; for if Jesus was merely a man, to claim that He was exactly like God in character would lay Him more open to the charge of ethical egotism than to claim that He was an eternal being one with the Father; for that must either be true or be characterised as insanity. The Fourth Gospel is perfectly clear that Christ claimed to be eternal, since He is there recorded to have said: "Before Abraham was, I am"; and the actual expression recalls the revelation made to Moses by God, "I am that I am": it is a claim to timeless being. Now, can that be supported from the Synoptics? There is no direct undisputed claim to pre-existence in the Synoptics, but surely the consciousness of being sent into the world, of coming into the world with a foreordained mission, involves pre-existence; especially when we consider that this mission was to redeem humanity, not merely by teaching men the true knowledge of God, but by dying for their ransom and the remission of their sins. The way in which Jesus speaks of His coming into the world, and of yielding up His life, entirely surpasses the normal human attitude to birth and death. If there is any lack of explicit clearness and dogmatic affirmation about all this, it is entirely explicable from the fact that Jesus desired it should be recognised and confessed by others, rather than merely accepted by them as a piece of information.

Neither does there seem to be any sign that the consciousness of who He was had been gradually

THE CONSCIOUSNESS OF CHRIST

arrived at; for it is not only declared at the Baptism, but, according to St. Luke, it was clear to Jesus when He was only twelve years old. When found in the temple and chidden by His parents for being lost, He replied, according to the most probably correct translation of the original, " Did you not know that I should be in My Father's house ? " This incident is distrusted by some, because it belongs to the Infancy narratives, and is unsupported in the other Gospels, but its *naïveté* is so like what we should expect from a child of that age, and it is almost inconceivable how such an incident could have been invented. Therefore we are driven to conclude that His filial relationship to His Father was a fundamental element in His consciousness, and that as soon as He came to self-consciousness He knew Himself to be the Son of God. The great difficulty about simply accepting this is that, while Christ seems to have been conscious of His divinity, it is difficult to regard His consciousness as in the strict sense divine ; and does not the one necessitate the other ? We have not only the years of infancy and childhood to consider, where a divine consciousness would make natural childhood and growth inconceivable, but we constantly have Christ asking questions in the Gospels as if He were not omniscient, and on one occasion He distinctly stated that a certain piece of knowledge was hidden from Him and known only to the Father : " But of that day or that hour knoweth no one, not even the angels of heaven, neither the Son, but the Father." But while this statement reveals that on this point Jesus was conscious of sharing the ignorance of created beings, that it should have been thus specified as something remarkable, bears witness not only to a superhuman, but to a super-angelic consciousness

THE CONSCIOUSNESS OF CHRIST

as normally His. The solution can again only be found by appealing to later developed doctrine, which implies that whatever Jesus was conscious of being, He was conscious of it in a human way, for His was a truly human mind. Although this is ecclesiastical doctrine, it is the only explanation which does justice to the facts of the Gospels, and which they implicitly demand. We must remember that even such high terms as " Son " and " Father " must be only human analogies of the divine relationship: their actual knowledge of one another is confined to themselves, as Jesus stated. But even this explanation seems difficult to many who devoutly desire to think rightly concerning our Lord's personality, for they have felt that if Jesus possessed even a human consciousness that He was divine, it would destroy the reality of His human experience; yet because there are times when He seems to move within the realm of a purely human consciousness, and others when not only does He appear to be conscious of being divine, but His consciousness itself seems divine, it has been suggested that His divine consciousness was only subconscious, while His normal consciousness was human. This is one of the very latest suggestions of modern Christology, but it has not won any great consent, perhaps because in the present state of psychology we hardly know what is meant by these terms, and the subconscious seems to contain so much that is also sub-human as well as superhuman. In the most recent psychology the subconscious stands for a species of mental activity which, although it may profoundly influence the conscious mind, is not able to be brought to consciousness, save by some process of analysis, and at the hands of another. But modern psychology has been compelled to make the further distinction of the pre-conscious, which is a state of knowledge which need not be present to the mind at any given time, but which can be brought to mind at will. It would be more than rash to use this at present indeterminate terminology for the definition of the mind and personality of Christ, but may we not use its aid to distinguish different states of consciousness in Christ ? He may not have been always conscious of His divinity, simply because He was not always thinking about Himself; in fact, He was generally thinking about others. Therefore His consciousness of His divinity may have been more in the nature of the pre-conscious, recalled or neglected at will. Moreover, we need to remember the divine consciousness itself may not be self-conscious in the same way that human consciousness is compelled to be; at least God's consciousness of Himself may be different from our consciousness of ourselves, and certainly different from our consciousness of Him. This may all be insufficient to prove, and still less to explain, the existence of a double consciousness in Christ, but it does show that such a thing is not inconceivable; and it seems therefore safe to argue that what Christ tells us of Himself shows He was conscious of Himself as divine, though this is expressed after the fashion of a human mind; nevertheless there are also signs in Him of the operation of a consciousness which is distinctly superhuman, and must be regarded as not only a conseiousness of divinity, but a divine consciousness.

We shall find an impressive confirmation of this conclusion if, instead of taking direct statements about Himself, we investigate what is involved in some statements which make no direct claim to divinity. It is important to notice that Jesus claims a relationship to humanity as unique as His relationship to God. He speaks of Himself as so integrated with our common humanity that to receive anyone in His name is to receive Him, nay, that to perform even the most common acts of kindness to our fellows is to serve Him, while to leave them undone is to neglect Him; and this to such a degree that our eternal destiny will be determined by our attitude to our fellows, because this reveals our attitude to Him. No other person has ever attempted to encourage and to elevate our common duty to our fellows by declaring that all service done to them was service done to him; still less to make this the material for determining our destiny, because it involves our ultimate attitude to God, our supreme Judge. In His sense of contact with humanity, the consciousness of Jesus reveals itself to be something entirely above a normal human consciousness. When again we turn to His lament over Jerusalem in which He says "*how often* would I have gathered thy children together as a hen gathereth her chickens," no number of unrelated visits to Jerusalem would suffice to fill out the meaning of this utterance, for it reveals a maternal attitude towards humanity which belongs to the absolute and eternal: we are moving within the realm of a consciousness that can only be characterised as essentially divine. This strictly divine consciousness can hardly be described as subconscious, according to its present connotation, since it can become conscious, although it is rarely revealed, and is most often only implicit.

The indisputable character of Christ's divine consciousness has so forced itself upon serious and impartial students of the Gospels that there seems now to remain open only one objection which can be urged against its truth; it involves a horrible estimate of the mentality of Jesus, but it is one which the modern mind has not shrunk from suggesting: it is that Jesus was misled in regard to His opinion of Himself; and since this opinion was evidently so immediate to His consciousness, it involves that on the point of His self-knowledge Jesus must be regarded as insane. There have been sad cases of persons who have thought themselves to be some great personage or even God, but this has been immediately recognised as insanity, because of its incongruity with the character and the general impression made by the person. But the one thing that Jesus does not do is to go about saying "I am God," which in face of this issue is more than fortunate; it is conclusive. The fact that His consciousness is divine only comes out by implication and indirectly, and always so modestly, quietly and naturally as to be entirely removed from the obsession of an insane person. We have to apologise for having to consider such a hypothesis, and indeed to ascribe insanity to Christ as an explanation of His consciousness is not only irreverent and blasphemous, it is much more like insanity in the persons who have proposed it.

It has been impossible to find any solution for the psychological facts which Christ's personality discloses save by having recourse to the apostolic doctrine and the dogmatic pronouncement of the Christian Church; but this is simply because they alone do justice to the facts, and because the facts inevitably necessitate them. Therefore we are bound to conclude that Christ's consciousness of Himself is only explicable as a consciousness that is both human and divine; it is the human consciousness of a divine person, and a divine consciousness operating within a human personality. It is on these lines that we must build our conception of His personality and the significance of His coming into the world.

VI

THE DEATH OF JESUS

THE Gospels make much of the death of Jesus. The actual space occupied in the Gospel record by the story of the last week of His life, and the details of the Passion narrative, are out of all proportion to the time which they occupied. It is only natural that the tragedy in which the life of Jesus ended should have produced a most profound impression upon the memory of that generation; and the cruelty, shame and suffering which the crucifixion involved would by their shock and horror engrave themselves deeply upon the feelings of those who loved and reverenced Christ.

But it has been thought that the attention given to the death of Jesus is due to the influence of the Apostle Paul, for his theories of sacrificial redemption led to his concentration upon the death almost to the ignoring of the life and teaching of Jesus. Consequently there has been an endeavour to shift the Pauline emphasis, and to redress the balance by concentrating upon the life and teaching of Jesus as containing in themselves sufficient significance for ethical inspiration and enough redemptive power to satisfy legitimate religious needs. It is believed, therefore, that the space given to the crucifixion has been due to a later interpretation of Christ's death, which can find no sanction in His own outlook and estimate. But an examination of the Gospels shows that, on the contrary, it was Christ's own attitude towards His death which provided the basis for the Pauline interpretation, that such an event must have struck any person with a historical sense as having profound significance, while the simple details of the passion narrative constitute a revelation and produce a redemptive effect. In the space they give to the death of Jesus, the Evangelists show their sense of proportion, and in their attitude towards it they only reproduce the place which it held in the consciousness of Christ Himself. It is not merely that the utter tragedy that Jesus should have come to such an end has dominated the mind and feeling of the Evangelists, because the apparent defeat of Christ's death would then have been obliterated by the triumph of the resurrection; but the crucifixion dominates the resurrection, which is memorable just because it is the resurrection of the Crucified who still bears the wounds of the cross. This emphasis on the death of Christ is therefore not due to a religious interpretation distorting the perspective of a historical life; it is a clear view of historic events giving rise to an inevitable religious interpretation of them.

The crucifixion of Jesus Christ must always remain one of the most startling and significant facts in human history. Whatever view may be taken of the personality and mission of Christ, the fact that such a person with such a purpose should have been brought to a violent and untimely end, is a fact that demands explanation and challenges thought. It is due to no accident, and not merely to the Church keeping alive the memory of Christ's death, that the Cross of Christ stands out as a turning-point in history, and a signpost for all time. As a historical fact, man is bound to take notice of it, for full as history is of tragedy, this is one of the greatest of tragedies, that so pure, wise and beautiful a soul should have been so foully done to death. The true historian is bound to take notice of it not merely as a fact, but also because it tells us a good deal about human history; it reveals in a most dramatic fashion the hidden motives that constantly control the human mind; it throws a sudden and disquieting light upon the constitution of human society and the consequences involved for any person who challenges and attempts to reform it; it lays bare the cowardice, injustice and cruelty of which even respectable, religious and good men are capable. But the death of Jesus does more than tell us about the secret currents of human history and the serious consequences of human blindness and frailty; it also tells us a good deal about Jesus Christ Himself, His purpose, and His teaching. Quite apart from a doctrinal interpretation, St. Paul is perfectly right, it is the death of Jesus that tells us the real meaning of His mission and brings out the importance of His teaching; for it is clear that if only Jesus had been willing to abandon His mission, moderate His claims, or even pursue His purpose along different lines, He could have escaped the cross.

And yet it was no mere accident, fatal combination of circumstances, morbid love of death and suffering or daring adventure that brought Jesus to His end. Indeed nothing is more difficult for us to state wherein lay the inevitableness of the cross, just because we have so little experience of sinlessness, perfect love of man, and complete fidelity to the light. And, therefore, impatient theorists, unwilling to admit the uniqueness of Christ and His acceptance of the cross as the means of redeeming the race, are compelled to seek for reasons and motives which altogether miss the point and find no adequate support in the Gospels. For instance, if the death of Jesus is looked upon merely as a tragic miscarriage of justice, a horrible accident of human circumstances which entangled an innocent soul, and therefore is nothing but a pure martyrdom, and an unhappy example of how things in this rough world work out, this explanation is crossed by the fact that Jesus clearly foresaw His own death, and, foreseeing it, not only did nothing to escape it, but deliberately walked into the zone of danger, and by His challenge and claims delivered Himself up into the hands of His enemies. And yet the moment it is recognised that Jesus foresaw, and by His words and actions brought about His own death, this raises difficulties for other minds who then conceive Jesus as merely carrying out a plan to which He believed He had been predestined by prophecy, or one which He had planned Himself, because He believed that nothing but His death would accomplish the redemption of humanity; and this inevitably gives them the impression of unreality and morbidity. But this can be countered by drawing attention to the fact that on more than one occasion Jesus deliberately evaded capture, and removed Himself from an area where danger openly threatened, and looked forward to His death with the horror and shrinking that culminated in the agony in Gethsemane. His death was therefore no morbid obsession and merely external necessity. Again, if we adopt the latest suggestion that the apocalyptic conception of the Messiah dominated the mind of Jesus, then we are driven to think of Jesus as unfortunately involving Himself in a conception which on the one hand enabled His enemies to prefer against Him the charge of blasphemy and of pretensions to an earthly monarchy, and on the other hand, forced Him to climb the cross in the hope that He might set in motion that catastrophic coming of the Kingdom which He thought His violent death might precipitate; and such a theory seems to imply that if only Jesus had not involved Himself in Messianic claims which were bound to be misunderstood, He could not have been touched, and that the apocalyptic dream which dominated His later ministry must be regarded as of the nature of a delusion by which He misunderstood God's method of governing and redeeming the world. And yet, this conception of Jesus being obsessed with apocalyptic dreams which could never be fulfilled, or of His making false claims owing to a mistaken conception that He was an apocalyptic Messiah, is so contrary to His calm outlook and clear rejection of the false Messianic notions of His time that it must be as decisively rejected as the other theories it has supplanted. The truth is that it is not possible to explain the attitude of Jesus towards His death and His recognition of the necessity for it unless we are willing to recognise that Jesus was a unique person with a unique mission, and the full explanation of His acceptance of the cross can only be found in the complete doctrine of His Person as human and divine, and in His death as being the only means of redeeming the world. Nothing less holds any clue to the psychology of Christ's mind, and the part He Himself played in the events that faced Him. We are to leave the doctrine of Atonement for exposition at a later stage, but while the purpose and motive of Jesus cannot be clearly and comprehensively set forth without that doctrine, it is also a fact that that doctrine has often deteriorated into legal, fictional and even unethical explanations, because the historical movement which brought Jesus to the cross has been overlooked, and the actual facts of the crucifixion have been forgotten. It is significant that the Church is committed to no theory of the Atonement, and that the Creed simply states that Jesus " was crucified for us under Pontius Pilate, He

THE DEATH OF JESUS

suffered and was buried," thus referring us to the historic fact for revelation and to the contemplation of the cross as the means of redemption. For what Calvary has done is to cut right down through all the complications of human circumstances, the disguises of human motives, the social structure and movements of mankind and reveal the fundamental sin that underlies and corrupts them all; and at the same time has revealed another movement which, if accepted by men, will purify and redeem the world. But at this point we do not appeal to the full doctrine of the Atonement, or even to the full doctrine of Christ's personality; it will be sufficient for us to show that Calvary and Christ's attitude to the cross demand them both, if we are going to penetrate to any understanding of either.

We begin, therefore, with the obvious fact that Jesus foresaw His death. How are we to account for this, and how soon did it dawn upon Him that He was to die? It has been suggested that at first Jesus thought that the Kingdom of God might be established by His teaching, which the simple-hearted people would be willing to accept; but that in the pursuit of His mission of preaching and healing He found Himself arousing enmity, that this soon developed to such an alarming extent that He began to sense danger, and that it was only then that He began to search around for some assurance that His death was necessary and might accomplish what His life had failed to do. And it was in this search that He was led to identify the career of the "Suffering Servant," portrayed in the Book of Isaiah, with the true Messianic rule of the Son of man. But the idea that Jesus was only gradually driven to consider the possibility of His having to die, and could only find a hope of its redemptive consequences by searching the Scriptures, or arguing with Himself, is overthrown by the fact that from the very beginning of His ministry He seems to have been aware that it would end in the cross. In the Fourth Gospel Christ's acceptance of the necessity of the cross is pushed back to the very beginning of His ministry, since there John the Baptist hails Him as " the Lamb of God that taketh away the sin of the world," which certainly involves the idea of the Lamb being slain as a sacrifice for that purpose; and in His conversation with Nicodemus Jesus sets forth the need for the Son of man being lifted up like the serpent in the wilderness in order that men should look to Him and be saved. This must not be rejected as due to the Evangelist unhistorically reading after events back into the past; for a similar expectation can be found in the Synoptics. As early as the second chapter of St. Mark, where we are moving in the sunny atmosphere of the Galilean days, and Christ is likening Himself and His disciples to a wedding party, He utters the warning that while He is the bridegroom, the day will come when the bridegroom will be taken from them. It should be noted that the first record of hostility is found almost immediately afterwards; the outward event therefore follows the premonition, so that the premonition is not based merely upon some external sign of impending danger. Nothing further is actually recorded in this Gospel about the necessity of His death until after St. Peter's confession, when immediately Jesus began to teach His disciples that the Son of man must suffer, and from now onward there is continual reference to this necessity as He makes His way to Jerusalem. It seems remarkable that no sooner should Jesus receive the clear confession of His Messiahship than that He should start to instruct His disciples that the Messiah must suffer.

THE DEATH OF JESUS

But the way in which the one immediately follows the other puts it beyond all doubt that Jesus was only waiting for the admission of the one in order to begin a new revelation, for both had always been clear to His mind. By this time it would have been indeed strange if Jesus had been unaware of the danger to which His life was exposed; there were the grumblings of the authorities and there was the fate which had already befallen John the Baptist; but His premonitions have already an expectation about them which amounts to a positive vision of what was actually to befall Him, the predictions of rejection and death developing, as they make their way to Jerusalem, into a detailed description of the mockery, shame and cruelty with which His death was to be accompanied. It is easy to suspect that all this has been worked up to correspond to the actual events, but if the details are objected to, there seems no reason why there should not be equal objection to any premonition of His death; this could not be justified, and the possibility of such prevision can only be denied to Jesus on theories which reject the supernatural and His divine consciousness. But the thing that has perplexed and puzzled many modern readers is the constant reference to the fulfilling of Scripture, which produces the impression that the only reason why Jesus had to die was because the prophets had said that He must; all this produces in their minds the idea that there was no natural necessity for Christ to die. Completely to clear this matter up we have only to turn to the purely historical side to see how it actually came to pass that Jesus was put to death.

Like most historical crises, the death of Jesus was the resultant of many crossing and converging movements, and is set in the midst of an extremely complicated set of circumstances. The Gospels make perfectly clear to us that the high ethical standard of His teaching reflected seriously upon the religious leaders of His times, while His performance of works of healing in defiance of regulations about Sabbath observance offended the Pharisees, who had erected the observance of the Law into an almost unbelievable rigour and value. The all-too-common motive of jealousy was aroused by Christ's popularity; this was combined with the wounded pride that His attacks upon hypocrisy created. These motives were both concealed and strengthened by intense religious convictions; for the Pharisees believed that the Kingdom of God would only come as men scrupulously kept the Law. Therefore, Christ seemed to be frustrating the redemption of the nation. It is also clear that Jesus exasperated another section by the height of His personal claims. When at the last Caiaphas adjured Him to declare who He was, the confession He extorted from Jesus enabled him to declare that He had blasphemed. Now a mere claim to be the Messiah could not have been condemned as blasphemous; it might be regarded as ridiculous on the part of a peasant, but although Jesus had disappointed even John the Baptist by spending His days succouring the sick and gathering about Him the outcasts, instead of setting some great national movement on foot, yet His miracles had been of such a character that many held that the Messiah could be expected to do no more. The Fourth Gospel brings out most clearly that it was not only the claim to be the Messiah, but it was the claim to stand in an intimate and unique relationship with God, which amounted to a claim to divinity, that incurred the most hostility. The answer of Jesus to Caiaphas admitted not only that He regarded Himself as the Messiah, but that He also claimed to be the Son of man who was to come and judge the world; this was quite sufficient to charge Him with blasphemy, however theatrical the high priest's abhorrence may have been, and however much he may have welcomed an admission which put Jesus into his hands. From the strict, Jewish point of view, for a man to claim divinity would, of course, be blasphemy. There is no doubt that the Old Testament prophecies had been advancing to a point where the Messianic person must be regarded as more than human, and that this was confirmed by the expectation that Jehovah Himself would come in person to save His people; but the Sadducees, who were the rulers of the Sanhedrin, had adopted liberal opinions, very largely given up the Messianic hope, were willing to make terms with this world and its ways, and were therefore opposed to the whole supernatural conception of things. Therefore the teaching of Jesus concerning Himself was running counter to theological conceptions; but this was complicated by the fact that while Jesus made such high claims, He preferred, and called upon others to follow Him in a lowly career, thus bracketing together divine dignity and human humility in a way that the religious leaders could not tolerate, partly because it seemed derogatory to divine majesty, but chiefly because it cast such a reflection upon their own pomp and pretensions. Lastly, Jesus had been arousing a great expectation among the common people that He was going to set up the Kingdom of God, which to them meant two things: the independence of the Jewish nation, and indeed their supremacy over all the nations of the world, and secondly, an era of social prosperity; and these two things involved in the minds of many the restoration of the Davidic monarchy, the overthrow of Rome by military means, and some kind of revolution in which the tyranny of the proud, the rich and the exactors would be overthrown. Therefore any claim to be the Messiah could easily be worked up into a charge of seditious conspiracy against the Roman authorities. It was this which Caiaphas was enabled to prefer when the case of Jesus was carried from the Sanhedrin to the Prætorium; Caiaphas was able to interpret Christ's claim to Messiahship as blasphemy before the ecclesiastical court and as sedition before the Imperial Court. However much Caiaphas may have known that Jesus was completely innocent of any military and political designs, he knew that the people were in a ferment, were roused by false expectations, that the extremely unstable social order was being endangered by the ministry of Jesus, and that this was bringing upon an always delicate situation the menace of Roman interference. Caiaphas must have known in his heart that all this was only an argument of governmental expediency; but he felt that the teaching of Jesus was religiously and socially unsettling, and Caiaphas and those who were in power did not want any kind of change which might deprive them of their prestige and position. It was an extremely complicated situation, but its complication reveals how human sin has cemented an order of thought, outlook and social structure, which makes the coming of the Kingdom of God, the actions of a sincere and earnest soul, nay the presence of God Himself, something which men fear, hate and cannot even tolerate.

This complication nevertheless straightened out into a compact combination of all parties against Jesus. The Pharisees were bitter nationalists who expected the Messiah to deliver them from the yoke of the foreigner and set them supreme over the rest of the world; and the attitude of Jesus, on the one hand, to Gentiles, and especially the Romans, and, on the other, to the outcasts and lawbreakers among their own people, whom they hated and despised as a real hindrance to the coming of the Kingdom, -outraged their blind, fierce, narrow religion, and aroused the hatred, envy and fear which spring from wounded pride and a repressed conscience. The Pharisees were at enmity with the Sadducees, whom they regarded as a set of worldlings and place-hunters; but while the Sadducees controlled the official appointments of the priesthood and the relations with the Imperial Power, the Pharisees were the popular leaders; and although they despised the common people, they were quite willing, if a favourable occasion should arise, to take advantage of their willingness to rebel against the Romans and bear the brunt of a violent revolution. This, however, was the one thing that the official party wanted to prevent, and although Jesus might have been a wonderful popular leader, He refused to put Himself at the head of any such project, while at the same time His demand for religious reality and His whole emphasis upon the supernatural character of faith was a reflection upon the worldliness and unbelief of the Sadducees. It is hardly likely that the combination of the religious and official parties could have secured the death of Jesus without at last the acquiescence of the common people. The part they played is less clearly discernible from the Gospel record, because it was a passive rather than an active one, but it is perfectly clear, that if there had not been some falling away of Christ's popularity among the common people, it would at least have been courting a revolution to have put Him to death. As it was, the authorities hurried things

THE DEATH OF JESUS

through so as to avoid any attempt to rescue Jesus on the part of any hot-headed Galileans who might be present at the Passover. But it is clear that the teaching of Jesus had gradually led to a popular disappointment; He could not join in their hatred of their Gentile oppressors, and especially of the publicans; neither would He promise a kingdom of prosperity that was not founded upon faith in God and the recognition of the brotherhood of all men. The pacifism of His teaching had alienated the revolutionaries, His refusal of the attempt to crown Him as a king had disappointed the nationalists, and His unwillingness to accept the protection of arms had caused Him to be regarded as an impractical dreamer. And therefore it was easy to work up the common people into a mob who were as violent in demanding His death as the authorities were determined to secure it; and there was little fear that there would be any popular movement to save Jesus once He was in the hands of His captors. Underneath all these complications of religious blindness, governmental expediency and popular disappointment, there can be discerned the indocility of pride, the love of power and the fear which it brings, and the impatience of idealism which stoops to seize unworthy weapons; and these are the fundamental sins of humanity which are always flowing underneath like hidden currents, but nevertheless dominate the motives of men and the movements of history; and it was these sins which made it impossible for Jesus to pursue His mission or even to be suffered to live for long in this world of ours.

From this short survey of the historical circumstances and political tendencies, we can the better discern the attitude of Jesus to the necessities which confronted Him. It would have been astonishing if

Jesus had not seen how soon His outlook would disappoint and exasperate almost everybody, and how the pursuit of His mission would only bring Him into danger. But it is important to notice that Jesus did everything not only to save Himself from any charge of being guilty of His own death, by making it perfectly clear that He would not lead any movement that was founded on the hate of enemies, that He intended to found a kingdom on a purely spiritual basis, and that, while He claimed divinity, He interpreted that as necessitating meekness of heart and lowly human service; but He also sought to save everyone else from the guilt of His death by trying to persuade them of the truth for which He stood, and win them to accept His Kingdom. It is this which accounts for the constant appeal to the fulfilment of Scripture. The current Messianic hope had deteriorated from the prophetic conception until the Messiah had become a purely nationalistic king, with no care or policy for other nations of the world save their subjection or destruction, an apocalyptic figure who was to set up the Kingdom of God by using the forces of nature to produce some physical upheaval, again solely with the Jews as the persons to be redeemed; and consequently, although this Messiah had become a portentous figure, He was not regarded as divine, and would still less be accepted as such if He worked by spiritual means and chose the humble and contrite for His friends. It was against this materialised, nationalised and wholly degraded conception that Jesus quoted the Scriptures in order to show that His view was the true one: namely, that the Messiah as David's Lord is a more than human figure, and there is committed to Him as the Son of man the more than human mission of the judgment of the world; that the Messiah must be lowlyhearted and be concerned for the outcasts of the social

THE DEATH OF JESUS

order and the lost souls among men; and, especially, that the world will not be ransomed from its bondage or redeemed from its sin without the Messiah's death, which alone could accomplish the repentance of the human mind, the conversion of the human heart, and the regeneration of human society.

It is obvious that if Jesus knew Himself to be sent into this world from the Father, He must have known that He came into this world to die, not only because to come into this world, constituted as it was, made His death humanly certain, but because this necessity was to be turned into a means of divine revelation, the remission of sins, and the redemption of the world.

The actual circumstances of Christ's death began almost immediately to have this effect. The attempt to overwhelm Jesus with shame and indignity only brought out the kingliness of His bearing, which even Pilate could discern; the cruelty of the scourging and the crucifixion only made more obvious the heroism of His heart and the courage of His character; while the mockery and hate hurled at Him only served to reveal that nothing could change His love of man or forfeit His forgiveness. Christ's bearing on the cross, and especially His prayer for others, converted one crucified beside Him to believe in His Kingdom, and the centurion who watched to declare He was the Son of God. St. Peter was able to charge upon the nation the crime of the brutal murder of one who was not only innocent, but the Holy One of God, and to declare that He bore our sins on the cross. And thus, as a mere historical and physical fact, the cross became a permanent memory in the mind of man, a fact which the passage of the centuries only sets in more arresting relief, and in contemplation of which the sincere conscience is moved to confess that here is revealed the malice and meanness of human sin, the willingness of Christ to suffer in order to save mankind, and therefore, to all who seek it, an assurance of the unchangeable love and freely offered forgiveness of God.

From the historical fact of Christ's death there flows, therefore, a movement which redeems history, by revealing the individual sin underlying social injustice and cruelty, bringing personal convictions of sin, repentance, and the assurance of forgiveness to the soul willing to consider the cross, awakening faith in Christ as the Saviour of the world, countering the force of evil custom by breaking the delusions which blind men and sundering their attachment to sin. So that the redemptive significance of Christ's death is not something read into it from alien notions or previous conceptions, but something discerned as historically flowing from it. It is not theological reflection which has led to concentration on the death of Christ, but the historic fact itself which has demanded reflection and produced the redemptive effect which is traceable to the cross as its simple and sufficient cause.

VII

THE RESURRECTION

THE Resurrection of Jesus Christ, if it is a veritable fact, constitutes a unique event in the history of mankind. The sepulchre of Jesus Christ is an empty tomb, and if that is a reliable proof that His body rose from the grave, then this world possesses no other monument of such profound and perpetual significance. But it is not merely as the resuscitation of a person's body from the grave, never to return thither, that the Resurrection of Christ holds such hope and meaning. We are not asked to believe in Christianity on the basis of some wonderful yet isolated fact. The Resurrection is to be considered as an incident congruous with the whole career of Jesus Christ: the fulfilment of His repeated promises and predictions, the natural and convincing proof of what He claimed to be, and, above all, the complete and triumphant reversal of the Crucifixion which men had designed to put an end to Him and His claims for ever. Therefore, when it is declared, as it has been, that Christianity is built upon an empty tomb, this is only to be accepted as a vivid and picturesque statement which is only half true; Christianity is not built only upon that, however wonderful it may be. And however mistaken and unnecessary the modern attempts to construct a Christianity without the Resurrection, or a faith in the risen, ascended and glorified Christ which should not involve an empty tomb, yet they have called attention to the fact that Christianity is founded on something more than a physical marvel: namely, on a marvellous personality whose career was accompanied by physical facts which are natural enough in connection with that personality, simply because that personality is itself supernatural. The acceptance of the Resurrection as a historical fact would carry with it no value for faith unless it was linked on to a conviction that Jesus taught the truth, involving the acceptance of Christ as all He represented Himself to be. For until we have seen the glory of God in the face of Jesus Christ, and in the Crucifixion the seal of the divine forgiveness, we are not concerned in the Resurrection, for that is significant as the Resurrection of the crucified Son of God, a fact therefore about one concerning whom we had already made up our minds. The attempt to dissociate belief in the historical fact of the Resurrection from that attitude towards Christ which constitutes faith, for whatever reasons undertaken, has had a salutary effect, not only in drawing attention to the vital essence of faith, but has even secured for the evidence a calmer investigation, which has made steadily for its rehabilitation. For when so much is made to depend upon a solitary marvel, fear is bound to creep in and create doubt; and it must be pointed out that God might have deemed it sufficient for a revelation of His nature and an assurance of His love to have ceased His incarnate manifestation without the Resurrection of Christ; or with the world's rejection of Christ God might have ceased any further attempt to win men back to Himself. But just as the Incarnation was necessary if man's belief in God was to be confirmed and raised to a higher level of knowledge and certainty, and just as Christ recognized that His miraculous works were the means of drawing attention to His claims, so God has

THE RESURRECTION

given us the Resurrection for the further confirmation of our faith, and also as a fact which compels men to consider the person of whom it is recorded.

Having admitted the necessity for a faith in Christ apart from the Resurrection, and having considered the hypothesis that God might have purposed this as sufficient, we can go on to consider the actual facts recorded, the psychological necessities demanded by the historical situation, and the more glorious fulfilment and assurance that the Resurrection brings. It is obvious that our Gospels, as they stand, would never have been written unless the Evangelists had been able to complete them with the story of the Resurrection. The Gospels contain constant predictions both of the Crucifixion and the Resurrection, generally together; and for the story to have finished with the one, and yet without the other, would not only have been an unfinished story, but a story which invited the rejection of Christ's claims. Even if we could eliminate these predictions as insertions made after the event, it is very doubtful, if the career of Jesus had ended with the Crucifixion, whether anyone would have taken the trouble to write the story of His life. So much was involved in His teaching and claims, that if His rejection and death as a criminal had been the last we had heard of Him, the world to-day would not have heard even that. And yet we have to consider the objections of modern scepticism that the story of the Resurrection is entirely inconceivable, or the suggestions of a radical criticism that it took its rise from a series of facts quite different from those presented to us in the closing chapters of the Gospels.

Fortunately, we have no longer to consider the theory that the story of Christ's Resurrection is a piece of sheer invention on the part of His disciples, whether motived by an attempt to satisfy their disappointed hopes or to foist upon the world a story from which they hoped to gain personal advantage. The modern attitude, however inadequate, will give no further hearing to any such hypothesis. The extremest radical criticism has reduced any such attempt to an absurdity by claiming that if the story of the Resurrection is an invention, why should not the Crucifixion, and indeed the whole story of Jesus or the existence of any such person, be regarded as an invention? The attempt to reduce the whole Gospel to a myth has been met even by unbelievers with the ridicule that it deserves; and yet the wild extravagance of this hypothesis should warn anyone against reducing the Resurrection to a myth.

The theory of sheer invention would involve that the disciples disposed of the body of Jesus. This theory was actually invented, according to St. Matthew, within a few days of the event. The Evangelist does not shrink from recording it, because he realized how absurd it was; and this has provided us with a valuable item of evidence, for it bears witness to the fact that the body had disappeared, and its disappearance had to be accounted for somehow. It was the first sceptical theory suggested, and if it is so absurd that its mere mention is enough to refute it, we shall probably find that all other theories which would explain away the Resurrection only operate in the same way, and show that the simple fact provides the only adequate cause for the story ever having been written. Nevertheless, we must take modern objections as we find them and face the fact that the story of the Resurrection has been challenged not only by confessed unbelievers, and by those who profess to believe in the moral mission of Jesus as of a sincere and enlightened person who taught some most valuable truths which men ought to believe and follow, but even by those who profess to believe that Jesus Christ was a true incarnation of God, and yet cannot accept the story of the Resurrection as recorded in the Gospels; and this, either on the idea that a purely spiritual faith must neither demand nor depend on anything physically marvellous; or because they feel the evidence for the Resurrection is too uncertain to demand faith in it; or because they have theories of the nature of the Resurrection manifestations which do not necessitate the resuscitation of Christ's body from the grave. The issue here is entirely dissociated from anything that would cast doubt on the good faith of the Evangelists, but it is believed their faith had a different basis than their narrative records. Those who propose an alternative origin for this faith do not hesitate to speak of the "Resurrection Faith," which they distinguish, however, from faith in the Resurrection. They believe that Christ rose from the dead, not only in the sense that His soul is immortal, but that He passed into heaven and received His rightful place in the glory of God; only they hold that this faith was created not by a physical or material event, but by something which they believe to be more fitting to the nature of that faith, namely, an interior revelation.

There are really five possible causes for the story of the Resurrection. The first is that of a sheer invention of the whole story, with whatever was necessary to obtain credence for it, engineered and foisted upon the world by the company of the disciples. This, however, as we have already seen, need not be further considered. The second theory is that the story of the Resurrection goes back eventually to an hallucination, probably started by Mary Magdalene, a person who is supposed to have been susceptible to mental derangement, since out of her, we learn, had been cast seven devils, and whose excited story spread expectation in the minds of others, and eventually created a series of mass hallucinations. This hypothesis is receiving less and less consideration. First of all, we are not perfectly sure to-day what is meant by hallucination; after all, a vision that is purely mental must have some cause, and it is never certain that the cause does not lie outside the person's mind who receives it, even if the cause only resides in some purely invisible realm. Moreover, the Gospel story gives little support to such a theory. It is the Fourth Gospel which gives us the record of the actual interview of the Risen Christ with Mary, and it indicates, what is common to nearly all the manifestations, that at first Mary did not recognize the person who spoke to her to be Christ at all, and until He called her by name, no doubt with some familiar intonation, she mistook Him to be the gardener. Nobody is going to suggest that it really was only the gardener, or suppose that there was a treble hallucination: first that she thought she saw a gardener, then that she thought that this non-existent gardener was Christ, and then that she thought that this wholly imaginary person spoke some extraordinarily transcendental words. Neither is there any indication that her report, or that of the other women who seemed to have seen Christ even before her, immediately set up anything like a receptive attitude in the minds of the disciples; they were not the kind of persons to give credence to what they felt to be idle tales, perhaps even the more so since they were told

THE RESURRECTION

them by women. Only slowly, and after repeated manifestations, did the eleven come to believe, Thomas only after a penetrating physical inquiry, while we are told that of the general body of disciples some were left at the manifestation on the mount in Galilee still unbelieving. The fact of the Resurrection had to make its way not among a mass of credulous and expectant minds, but steadily against minds depressed, unexpectant and very slow to be convinced. Hallucinations notoriously wear off as time passes, so that these men would have gradually doubted instead of growing surer as time went on.

The third theory to be considered is that the Resurrection was originally a growing conviction that Jesus was spiritually alive. This conviction was a true one; but either because it produced striking visualizations or some form of vision which had, however, no physical reality, or through the growth of legend, it took the form which it now wears in the Gospel story. This theory entails that when the disciples had time to consider all the facts, they recalled how Jesus had promised to return to them, and they began to feel His presence, just as Christ may to-day be felt near in moments of great devotion, or in public worship, and especially at the Eucharist. It is questionable whether the disciples had the type of mind which could be satisfied by this kind of evidence; and probably that interior sense of Christ's presence is much more of a modern growth, due to the cultivation of spiritual sensibility, than is often realized. Moreover, it is difficult to imagine how the transition between that experience and the concrete stories of the Resurrection in the Gospels was actually made. But it has been suggested that in some of the stories we get signs of this more spiritual conception, whereas in others we get a much more physical presentation. For instance, in some stories Jesus comes into a room where the doors and windows are all shut, or vanishes away, as at the meal at Emmaus; whereas in others He has a body which He invites to be handled and which can partake of food; and finally, in order to convince materially minded people, we get the story of the empty tomb and of a body literally resuscitated. But unfortunately for this theory we do not find these different types of idea in different stories, but combined by the same writer in the very same story. The figure that vanished from their side at Emmaus had already walked and talked with the two disciples for a long part of the journey. It is the very figure who suddenly appears in their midst who invites the disciples to see His hands and feet and handle Him and give Him something to eat. It is the mystical and spiritual author of the Fourth Gospel who gives a most vivid and detailed account of the finding of the tomb with the body gone, and yet with the clothes left behind, and, apparently, undisturbed as if the body was still within them, but had vanished by a kind of dematerialization. Yet this same author tells the story how this same figure was not merely discerned in some dim and misty fashion on the shore when the disciples were returning from their fishing, but sat down to a meal with them which He Himself had prepared. Moreover, this theory demands that the conviction of Christ being still alive must have dawned gradually; but the Christian Church has an institution which goes back, according to the Acts of the Apostles, to the very beginning, namely, the institution of Sunday, which was observed as the festival of Christ's Resurrection. This is not only a definite day, but the day was chosen in distinction from, and as a substitute for, the Jewish Sabbath, was invested with a good deal of the older festival's original sanctity, and chosen because on that day Christ rose from the dead. A good deal has been made of the fact that St. Paul, who is, of course, our first documentary witness of the Resurrection, links on the story of the appearances with the appearance to himself. It is argued that this was a purely spiritual appearance; and, moreover, that since St. Paul taught that flesh and blood could not inherit the kingdom of God, he did not know of the story of the empty tomb, and could have had no use for a material appearance. But according to the story of Christ's appearance to St. Paul, as given in the Acts of the Apostles, it was not a purely spiritual vision, but a physical manifestation, overpowering in its glorious light. While St. Paul certainly did not hold the glorified body to be a body of flesh, he held that it was a transformation of that body, and he still calls it a body. Moreover, even if this could be pressed, we should still have to account for how the Gospel story then arose; it would seem to be quite unnecessary to condescend to this materialization if St. Paul was already preaching, and with success, a purely spiritual or non-material resurrection. Most modern critics recognize that that which comes first in the Gospel story, namely, the discovery of the empty tomb, must be the real origin of the story; and if the Resurrection was preached in Jerusalem within fifty days of the Crucifixion, there would have been many attempts to disprove the story by recovering the body of Jesus; and since the tomb was a well-known spot, however rapidly decomposition had taken place, the condition of the tomb would surely have provided evidence sufficient to discredit the story. An attempt has, however, been made to account for the story of the empty tomb without the resurrection of the body of Jesus. It must be reckoned as a most ingenious speculation, but it has only to be stated to appear hopelessly improbable. The theory is that the women came to the tomb in the early morning, before it was light, mistook an empty tomb where some person was engaged at work, who, knowing their quest, said to them, "He is not here; come, see the place where He lay," and was about to conduct them to the right tomb; but they, misunderstanding his meaning and taking him to be a heavenly visitant saying that Christ had risen, immediately fled from the place with the astounding news. It involves, as will be recognized, that not one of the incredulous hard-headed disciples, and no unbeliever, went to see if there was the slightest truth in the women's story, but accepted it without further inquiry. This must be surely the last desperate attempt to find a different origin for the Resurrection story than that the Gospels give.

But there is a fourth way of accounting for the Resurrection manifestations which draws its material from the analogy of spiritualistic phenomena. F. W. H. Myers, in his book on Human Personality, declared that but for the evidence brought forward in his work, in a hundred years hence no one would be found believing in the Resurrection, whereas now in a hundred years hence no one would be found disbelieving in it. This is not the place to discuss the reality, truth and nature of the phenomena alleged to occur at spiritualistic séances; from rappings, sounds and lights, these have now advanced not only to materializations, but the creation of their form has been photographed and the material denominated as ectoplasm. But even if credence could be given to these phenomena, and there remain many who have investigated the whole subject and are yet entirely unconvinced that the phenomena are genuine or the work of departed spirits, and although it may be admitted that the literature gathered round this subject has created an atmosphere in which it is much more easy to accept the Resurrection, it must be pointed out that there is a vast difference between the two classes of manifestations. There is first of all the story of the empty tomb, which spiritualistic phenomena do not require. Secondly, there is the fact that in the Gospel records we have nothing like the atmosphere of the séance: there is no recognized medium, many of the manifestations occur in the open or in broad daylight, so far from there being an immediate recognition of the person materialized, the Risen Christ is constantly mistaken for some other person, until by voice or gesture, the display of the wounds in His body, or by the character of His communications, He is unmistakably identified. The Gospel record also shuts out any idea that Christ's manifestations were simply what are called apparitions, for the reality of which there is now a vast accumulation of reliable evidence. These apparitions seem to be caused by a telepathic projection from the dying person to the recipient mind of someone perhaps definitely thought of at the time. In accordance with this idea such projections might have been made from the Cross and received by the fugitive disciples some time after; which would explain the delay in their reception as well as the references to the Risen Christ bearing the marks of the Crucifixion. But of course such apparitions would not prove even the survival of Christ after His death, and between apparitions of this character, in which the recipient immediately knows that the person so appearing is dead, and the Gospel record with its triumphant conviction that Christ is alive, there is a gulf which nothing can bridge.

All these attempts fail to give any psychological or rational account of the origin and development of faith in the Resurrection; to account for the Gospel story being founded on any such explanations as we have been considering would entail that these records are nothing but an unexamined and uncritical deposit of unchecked legend; whereas the growth of such a legend would not only have had to make its way against the knowledge of the original disciples that something quite different was the origin, but would also have had to meet the confident denial of their opponents. When we consider the vivid and asseverated testimony of the Fourth Gospel, we are compelled to accuse either the fourth Evangelist himself or some apostolic intermediary of deliberate and shameless invention; and this even the most radical criticism will no longer consider.

We are therefore left facing the final explanation, which is that of the story as plainly told in the Gospels. But if the alternatives are historically, critically and psychologically improbable, can it be held that the Gospels provide us with a consistent and credible account of the Resurrection? It may readily be admitted that the four narratives contain many difficulties. There is, first of all, the fact that in our two oldest and most reliable manuscripts the narrative in St. Mark ends without any actual manifestation of the Risen Christ. That the closing verses of St. Mark should be missing has naturally raised suspicions, either that the narrative ended here, or that it was destroyed because it was unsatisfactory; but these suspicions

THE RESURRECTION

are really groundless. The narrative cannot have ended where it does in the two manuscripts; no Greek sentence could have been ended in this way: it has been broken off. It is more than likely that St. Mark's ending, like the rest of his Gospel, is embedded partly in St. Matthew and St. Luke; this Gospel, like the others, looks forward to a triumphant manifestation, and it would never have been written if that account could not have been appended. The end of St. Mark's narrative which is found in the majority of manuscripts probably came from another hand than that of the original Evangelist's; but if that is so it only makes it an additional witness, for although it looks somewhat like a compilation from material found in the other Gospels, there is late manuscript evidence that it was actually written by one of the original disciples, named Ariston. There is a further difficulty in fitting in the various appearances, and determining the order of events, the number of angels seen at the tomb, and the locality where the manifestations took place; but these can actually be fitted in if we allow for a narrative which is not meant to be a scientific account written in order to establish belief; for it must be remembered that belief in the Resurrection must have existed for at least twenty years without any published record. The proclamation of the Resurrection by apostles and evangelists, its centrality to the Gospel, the observance of Sunday and the establishment of the Christian Church, are the real historical evidences for the Resurrection, and not mere documents, however early or authentic.

A further difficulty is found in the attempt to construct a consistent theory of the objective nature of the appearances. It would be a great mistake to build too much upon anything in our present knowledge as giving us a scientific explanation of the risen body of Christ; but if we combine whatever truth and reality lie behind the accumulated evidence of psychic phenomena, together with the theory of the constitution of matter as resting upon an invisible basis, perhaps of the nature of electrical energy and conceivably transformable into differing visible presentations or degrees of materialization, then we have material which enables us to conceive at least the possibility of the Resurrection; for while it is ultimately a fact belonging to the spiritual and supernatural realm, in so far as it is a manifestation within the physical and natural realm it must use natural material according to the laws of its constitution. But it should be noted that the Resurrection is not so much a display of psychic as of moral power; Christ is said to have been raised from the dead by the spirit of holiness, and it is an important fact that the Risen Christ appeared to none save disciples: there was no attempt made to convert the outside world.

The Resurrection must rest on some relation, first, between material appearances and psychic force, and, second, between psychic power and that moral realm which is the ultimate reality; and we may see in the Resurrection first the transformation of the ordinary physical body into a psychic body, able to be visible or invisible and to assume different forms at will, then a transformation into some glorious body of light, as seen by the Apostle Paul, and at last to that moral supremacy which can only be symbolically set forth in the doctrine that Christ is seated at the right hand of God. If the Resurrection is a revelation of the spiritual realm, made within the visible and physical world, it must partake of them both; and if our knowledge of both or either realms, and the laws of their connection, interpenetration and reaction, is imperfect, we should expect to find some items in such a manifestation mysterious, unintelligible or, to us, even contradictory. Therefore it is wiser to leave the whole Gospel story as it stands, and not cut out this or that incident as mistaken. We have seen that growing scientific knowledge and alleged psychic phenomena make some things look intelligible which were once inconceivable: and if there are some things we can now accept because of new knowledge, further knowledge may confirm the consistency of the whole story. The Resurrection has often been doubted, not so much because we were not in possession of knowledge which now makes it more conceivable, but its doctrinal significance has not been understood, and therefore to some persons in our generation it has seemed to be unnecessary and a condescension to materialism. But the Christian religion is not a purely spiritual religion, it is the religion of the Incarnation; it reveals that the material is not opposed to the spiritual, which can become by a transforming process its perfect instrument. Moreover, the Christian religion is a religion of redemption. Even though Christ had manifested the forgiveness of God by the spiritual attitude with which He faced and bore the Cross, this would have left a very incomplete and shadowy assurance if it had not been confirmed by the Resurrection. To show how truly Christ forgives men for the crime by which He was hurried out of this world, He comes back again and by His revisiting us, as well as by His further instruction, confirms and completes the incarnate revelation which the Crucifixion seemed to interrupt and defeat. The nature of the Resurrection appearances shows how the most spiritual and exalted life does not despise material things, how He who is now declared by the Resurrection to be highly exalted yet stooped to wear forms which were mistaken for lowly and ordinary persons, and even condescended to perform the most lowly services; thereby assuring us that God is uttermost forgiveness, to be looked for and served in our common humanity and concerned in all our ordinary life and necessities.

VIII

THE VIRGIN BIRTH

IF the Gospel records are taken as a whole, they unquestionably begin and end in miracles which are congruous with the career and person of Christ. The Resurrection is a stupendous miracle; that Christ should be born of only one parent is miraculous enough, though not perhaps of such a stupendous character, since it is not in the nature of things so inconceivable, even though it may be more unparalleled than the Resurrection; for we have stories of persons being raised from the dead in the Old Testament, as well as similar miracles performed by Christ. But while the attitude of the modern mind towards the Resurrection is perceptibly altering, owing partly to the attention given to psychical phenomena, which, although not proven, or strictly bearing upon the Resurrection, have affected the atmosphere through which the Gospel phenomena are viewed; and still more to the psychological impossibility of accounting for the Resurrection story, since it is difficult to conceive how the Gospels would ever have been written, or the Christian faith proclaimed, unless the Resurrection was a fact, for it permeates and forms the foundation of the Apostolic faith; nevertheless the attitude of the critical mind towards the Virgin Birth remains suspicious and still unconvinced. This is because it regards the evidence for the Virgin Birth as much weaker than the evidence for the Resurrection, and it believes the story can be more easily accounted for by the growth of legend, the influence of pagan mythology or by adaptation to Hebrew prophecy, than by assuming the Virgin Birth to be an actual historical fact. There also undoubtedly enters into the modern attitude a dislike for what it conceives to be the implications of the story, as well as its general objection to everything supernatural.

Christian theology must be willing to consider every historical and scientific fact that is brought to light, for all facts are God's facts; and God's facts need only the evidence of truth and not the decoration of legend. Therefore, although the Church's belief in the Virgin Birth assumes the veracity of the Gospel records, has been dogmatically affirmed in the Creeds, and is embodied in the Te Deum and in many early and popular Christian hymns, these considerations cannot be used to repress discussion or to influence conclusions. Moreover, it would be well to recognize that belief in the Incarnation is not necessarily bound up with the acceptance of the Virgin Birth. There are modern scholars who profess most emphatically that they believe that Christ was God Incarnate, but who declare that they are unable to accept the evidence for the Virgin Birth as sufficient; and although the rejection of the Virgin Birth has often been followed by the abandonment of any real belief in the Incarnation, this cannot be claimed as a necessary consequence. Moreover, there are the Mohammedans and heretical sects within Christianity who have definitely or implicitly denied the Incarnation while retaining belief in the Virgin Birth. But we cannot obtain a fair discussion of the subject while any sort of confusion remains, or if there is any fear that the rejection of the historicity of the Virgin Birth would necessarily carry with it abandonment of belief in the Incarnation; though we may eventually discover

THE VIRGIN BIRTH

that the two things are more bound together than has always been realized, and it may come to be understood that the Incarnation demands the Virgin Birth. But, as we have seen, a Virgin Birth does not demand an Incarnation, so that it is on the Incarnation rather than on its mode that faith ultimately rests. Unfortunately it is necessary to refer to another confusion which is widespread and is found in the most unexpected places. Pope Pius IX in 1854 decreed that the Virgin Birth of our Lord demands the Immaculate Conception of Mary; whether this is to be regarded as a dogmatic pronouncement that binds all the faithful, or whether there is any evidence for it that makes it a scriptural or reasonable dogma is not at this moment under discussion; but it is necessary to point out that the Virgin Birth and the Immaculate Conception are two entirely different things. The Virgin Birth solely concerns the birth of our Lord; the Immaculate Conception is a doctrine concerning the conception of Mary, which although due to ordinary human generation, is declared to have been miraculously excluded from the stain of original sin.

But while we agree that no discussion must be burked and no fact repressed, has any fact been brought to light by modern discussion which is sufficient to discredit the witness of the Gospels to the Virgin Birth? Suspicions have been roused by various discoveries and still more by suggestions that have been made, not only in modern, but in primitive times, and these must be given the fullest weight, and even the most minute discussion, if it is to be shown that the fact of the Virgin Birth remains unshaken, worthy of acceptance and capable of being imposed as an article of faith demanded by the Church. The first point that is made against the doctrine of the Virgin Birth is that its support in the New Testament is meagre, and is confined to only two authorities, namely, the Gospels of St. Matthew and St. Luke. It is assumed that it was unknown to the Apostle Paul or to St. John, since it is not mentioned in the writings ascribed to them. But, considering the cause and character of the New Testament writings, it must be admitted that a fact like the Virgin Birth not being referred to by a writer is no proof that it was unknown to him; and even if the fact of the Virgin Birth were unknown to some writers, that does not discredit the knowledge which other writers affirm. There are many facts in the Gospels which rest on literary evidence no stronger than that which supports the story of the Virgin Birth. If, as is widely assumed by criticism, both St. Luke and St. Matthew simply inserted the Marcan narrative into their own Gospel, that does not constitute a threefold witness, for mere copying does not increase the amount of evidence. But if anything can be certain in New Testament criticism, it is that St. Matthew and St. Luke are entirely independent of one another in their opening chapters, since in their stories of the infancy they contain many things which we find difficult to reconcile. Yet whatever differences the narratives contain, they agree in their witness to the Virgin Birth. On this point, therefore, we have a dual witness of peculiar strength. Further, the lack of reference in the rest of the New Testament is not so absolute as might be assumed. There were obvious reasons why the story of the Virgin Birth should not have been made known until somewhat late, or put forward as a piece of public news. It might only have led to such aspersions upon the honour of Mary as we find embodied in the Talmud. All that we can reasonably demand is that there shall be nothing contradictory of the Virgin Birth in the rest of the New Testament. This we actually find, and, in addition, what may be regarded as implicit confirmations of it. For instance, St. Mark's Gospel naturally has no reference to the Virgin Birth, since it begins with the story of the Baptism; but it is almost startling to discover that St. Mark never refers to any father of Jesus, and while the parallel passage in St. Matthew reads, " Is not this the carpenter's son ? " and in St. Luke, " Is not this Joseph's son ? " St. Mark has " Is not this the carpenter, the son of Mary ? " This looks like something more than a mere testimony from silence. Again, in the Fourth Gospel, we have a reference to the spiritual birth of Christians, which, according to overwhelming textual authority, reads, " Which were born, not of blood, nor of the will of the flesh, nor of the will of man." The analogy would be all the more apt if it was known to the Evangelist and to his readers that Jesus was virgin-born. And a Latin manuscript, whose testimony has been made much of because it happens to omit the verse in St. Luke's narrative which is important in this connection, " And Mary said unto the angel, How shall this be, seeing I know not a man ? " at this point contains the variant which would be an explicit testimony to the Virgin Birth, for it reads, "*Who* was born, not of blood, nor of the will of the flesh, nor of the will of man " ; and some scholars have suggested that this may be the original text, even though this is the only testimony for it. St. Paul certainly has no reference to the Virgin Birth, but from the nature of his Epistles and the general absence of detail about the life of Christ this would not be remarkable; but in writing to the Galatians he does say, " God sent forth His Son, born of a woman "; this by no means necessitates a reference to the Virgin Birth, but it is not the only Hebrew way of referring to human birth, and at any rate it does nothing to deny it, as any other expression for human birth might have done.

It is, however, felt by some that the stories of the Virgin Birth in St. Matthew and St. Luke are inherently suspicious, since both the genealogies are traced through Joseph, and afterwards in these two Gospels Joseph is called the father of our Lord; and it has therefore been suggested that both these Gospels were originally without the narrative of the Virgin Birth. There is absolutely no documentary evidence that the Gospels were ever published without the infancy narratives, and the references to Joseph being the father of Jesus are quite natural to the Gospel narrative, for this simply records what was generally assumed, or was adopted because any other usage would have entailed constant and awkward explanations. It has been pointed out, however, that the testimony to the Virgin Birth in St. Luke actually depends on two verses only, i. 34 and iii. 23; but only of the first of these is there any evidence for omission, and that only in one manuscript, the Latin version mentioned above, which would carry no authority on any other peculiarity, in which as a matter of fact it abounds, while this particular omission is easily accounted for by an accident in copying, frequently made and known as dittography. But more serious weight has been attached to the fact that a very early and very important manuscript of the Syriac version, known as the Codex Sinaiticus, reads in the genealogy of St. Matthew, i. 16, " Joseph begat Jesus." This reading seems to underlie a few manuscripts of the old Latin version and a small group of late Greek manuscripts. It is possible that this might represent the original text, for the genealogy as traced in St. Matthew really demands that Jesus should be reckoned as the son of Joseph, as legally He was. Yet, according to the general principles and canons of textual criticism, the small family of manuscripts which contain this variant would, on other matters, carry no weight whatsoever. It is only because of the great doctrinal importance of the passage that what is from the textual point of view only an interesting variant has drawn such attention to itself. Moreover, the chief manuscript in which these variations occur actually contains an additional witness to the Virgin Birth; for the Syriac Codex not only inserts between " Joseph begat Jesus " the words "to whom was betrothed Mary, *the* Virgin," but also omits the verse in St. Matthew i. 25, which declares that Joseph knew not Mary until she brought forth a son; so that the writer of this manuscript thought of Mary not only as a Virgin, but as *the* Virgin, and hesitated to admit anything that seemed to cast doubt upon her perpetual virginity. It can be nothing more than a suggestion, but one that seems in every sense likely, and in some sense is even necessary to assume, that the story in St. Matthew must have been derived from Joseph, whereas the story in St. Luke must have been derived from Mary; and, all things considered, the comparative lateness of the record and lack of reference to the story are natural and to be expected. Therefore we can say that, as far as textual testimony is concerned, the Gospel record is overwhelming and unshakable.

Modern criticism, however, tries to penetrate behind the text by what is called historical criticism, though there it embarks upon a series of suspicions and surmises which, if they cannot always be disproved, can also, in the nature of the case, never be proved. We can only have recourse to the general canons of psychological probability, and if the story cannot be more easily accounted for by some origin other than that of fact, then the fact must be taken to be the only possible explanation. Other causes for the origin of this story have, however, been put forward, and they must now be examined. The first is that the story is due to a desire to fulfil the prophecy contained in Isaiah vii. 14, " Behold, a virgin shall conceive and bear a son, and shall call his name Immanuel." What was actually meant when the prophet uttered these words to Ahaz has provoked considerable speculation, but little agreement has been reached or a satisfactory clue discovered. It is pointed out, however, that the actual Hebrew word used need not mean " virgin," though it does most naturally imply a young unmarried woman. Jewish commentators do not, therefore, generally take the original meaning to be a promise of a virgin birth, or regard it as a prediction of the Messiah, although by the time the Septuagint translation was made, the Hebrew word was translated by a Greek word which unambiguously means a virgin. But, in any case, it is difficult to see how this prophecy could have given rise to St. Matthew's story; moreover, St. Luke does not quote this prophecy; and, while Christian commentators may rightly hold that there was no true fulfilment of Isaiah's words without the Virgin Birth, it is certainly far easier to believe that the fact recalled the prophecy than that the prophecy created the story.

But it is frequently alleged that the idea of a virgin birth is common enough in heathen religions,

THE VIRGIN BIRTH

and is a frequent motive in pagan myths; so that it is no wonder that the story should have arisen in Christianity. But, in reality, this is just the difficulty; for even if it were a frequent incident in pagan mythology, that would hardly have recommended the story to the Jewish mind. Moreover, if we examine the alleged instances of virgin birth elsewhere, they turn out to be anything but virgin births, but instead, more often divine rapes conceived after a grossly sexual fashion. The alleged virgin birth of Buddha occurs in a very late record, probably later in origin than, and perhaps influenced by, the Christian story. In the earlier stories of the Buddha his mother was certainly not a virgin, and even in the late story it must be taken as a symbol not even meant to imply a virgin birth.

Others have thought, however, that the poetic impulse is sufficient to account for the story. We need not dispute that the Nativity stories are poetic; they are told with a lyrical touch, and yet with fine restraint, as a comparison with the Apocalyptic Gospels makes us aware. If they were sheer creations, then they surpass anything that the Greek writers, with their vast mythological material and their great poetic genius, have produced. But the poetry is due, not to the telling of the story; that is very matter of fact and unadorned; but to the facts themselves. And if the motive of the story of the Virgin Birth had been merely to express in poetic form the truth that all birth can be pure and every soul is begotten of God, it was really a most unfortunate line to take deliberately to exclude the male parent, for owing to wrong interpretations of why this was necessary, the truth the story was supposed to embody has been completely confused and lost sight of.

THE VIRGIN BIRTH

Finally it has been suggested that the story may have arisen in Essene circles, where marriage was looked down upon and abstained from. But the appeal to Essene influence, a favourite method in theosophical reconstructions of Christianity, must be classed among mere vagaries; there is absolutely no sign of any such influence in the New Testament, and, as a matter of fact, no reference to the Essenes at all. Therefore we are bound to say that the simple fact is the only explanation that at present holds the field.

But there has been something in the last two suggestions of an alternative source for the story of the Virgin Birth which demands a consideration of its doctrinal significance; for it is the misunderstanding, or perhaps the absence of any clear idea of its doctrinal significance, which has done more than anything else to lay the story open to attack; and it has often aroused dislike in certain minds because it has seemed to cast an aspersion upon the ordinary means of conception. The addition to the scriptural doctrine of the Virgin Birth of the ecclesiastical doctrine of the Immaculate Conception has somewhat increased this suspicion; but it is a wholly mistaken inference from either. To declare marriage impure or the procreative act between the sexes a sin would be a most serious heresy; and the idea that the mere exclusion of the male parent would eliminate the inheritance of sinful tendencies is an idea which the most advanced feminist would honourably repudiate and no Catholic theologian would dream of arguing. Indeed, the doctrine of the Immaculate Conception only emphasizes that something more than the mere exclusion of the male element in conception would be necessary. That there was a special preparation through history for the body which Christ was to

THE VIRGIN BIRTH

assume is a scriptural and natural idea, and the fact that sin has taken such occasion in the intercourse between the sexes to make the human side of birth so often unworthily motived and morally degrading does show the necessity for some purification of our human begetting, if it is to be worthy of the Incarnation. The late ecclesiastical doctrine of the Immaculate Conception seeks actually to provide for that in its declaration that Mary was conceived without original sin; which after all is only an anticipation of what, according to a much more widely accepted belief, is given to all children by Baptism. It need not be denied that many unfortunate ideas and expressions have been in vogue about the need for the Virgin Birth, but it may be stated without fear of challenge from dogmatically defined faith that it has nothing whatever to do with the moral unsuitability of ordinary marriage. The reason for the Virgin Birth is to be sought primarily in the ecclesiastical definition of what constituted the Person of Jesus Christ. This we shall have occasion to examine and compare with the scriptural doctrine at a later occasion; but at this point it may be stated that, according to the formulated theological doctrine, the Second Person of the Blessed Trinity was incarnate in Jesus Christ; that Person therefore took the place in Jesus Christ which the ego takes in an ordinary human being. Now ordinary human birth brings into existence a new individual, human person; therefore, in the case of the Incarnation ordinary birth would have given us a new human person plus the Second Person of the Blessed Trinity in the same individual; we should then have had a case of double personality: the Eternal Person of the Word and the individual person born in time. This would have landed us in the position which is known as Nestorianism and has been dogmatically declared to be heresy. Why it was denounced as heresy will be discussed in its proper place. But it may be noted here that, between the divine Person and the human mind and physical flesh He assumed, we should then have interposed a human person; and this would give us nothing more than the indwelling of a human person by God, such as is open to any religious soul, and this would have been no advance upon the prophetic mediation of the Divine Word, would not be a true incarnation of the Divine Word, and would not give us an immediate revelation of God in humanity. It was necessary for the revelation of Himself and the redemption of our race that God should assume a human body and rational soul, and therefore that He should take flesh of a mother; but if there had been the ordinary human conception and begetting, then, unless there had been some intervention, or some breach of God's ordinary co-operation with the human element in conception, there would have been an individual human person alongside of and merely indwelt by the divine Person. Therefore if ecclesiastical theology is correct, it would almost seem as if a true incarnation could only take place by means of a virgin birth; at any rate these conceptions lift the whole necessity for the Virgin Birth on to a different level, where it is free from false ideas that have done much to hinder belief in it.

It is probable, however, that many persons are prevented from giving a fair consideration to the Virgin Birth because of what they consider the undue exaltation of Mary to which this event has inevitably contributed. Whatever the popular exaggerations or misunderstandings have been, and whatever dangerous tendencies towards Mari-

THE VIRGIN BIRTH

olatry have been developed, these must not hinder us from giving to Mary the place that is rightfully hers. That she should have been selected to be the earthly mother of the Eternal Word is an honour which lifts her to a place which no other human being can hold. By all definition and explicit acknowledgment, Mary is no more than human, and separated from the Divine by the same gulf that separates us all; but she is the "most blessed amongst women," and all generations who realize what she has done for us agree to call her "blessed"; for while none but Christ could open to us the gates of heaven, not only did God choose her to be the mother of His Son, but by her meek assent to God's will, it was she who opened the gates of earth to the coming of our Lord. And although there have been considerable additions in ecclesiastical legend and popular devotion to the scriptural record of Mary's career, there is sufficient in the New Testament to claim for her not merely the motherhood of our Lord, but a most intimate relation with His redeeming work; for Simeon's words, "A sword shall pierce through thine own soul," give her a share in His Passion; she is found standing by the Cross at last, and she was certainly with the company in the Upper Room in the days of preparation that fell between the Ascension and Pentecost. But students of the New Testament often feel themselves hindered from recognizing any spiritual intimacy between the Virgin Mary and her divine Son because the Gospels seem to hint that she failed to understand Him and was even hostile to His ministry. While there are words of Jesus which seem almost to repudiate her maternal position, on examination this will, however, be found to be a mistaken conclusion. For instance, on one occasion when a woman in the crowd cried out, "Blessed is the womb that bare Thee, and the breasts which Thou didst suck," Jesus said, "Yea rather, blessed are they that hear the word of God and keep it." But this saying only brings out the real significance of Mary's motherhood: what Jesus repudiates is the mere physical maternity, what He praises is that obedience to the will of God which was the sole cause of Mary's maternity. Therefore, this emphasis on spiritual obedience, while itself a testimony to the Virgin Birth, admits into an analogous spiritual position all who, like her, meekly submit to the divine will. This interpretation throws light in turn upon another passage. On one occasion we are told that the friends of Jesus sought to restrain Him because they thought Him beside Himself, and then, shortly afterwards, we are told that His mother and His brethren stood without, seeking for Him to come to them; on hearing that, He turned to those who were listening to His words and said, "Who is my mother and my brethren? And looking round on them which sat round about Him, He saith, Behold my mother and my brethren! For whosoever shall do the will of God, the same is my brother, and sister, and mother." There is no necessity to identify those who sought to restrain Him with His mother who was seeking Him, and the words of Jesus on this occasion only emphasize what we have seen to be the true meaning of the other passage we examined; it is a disclaiming of mere physical relationship, for our Lord's relationship to His mother and His brethren was not on the same level as that of an ordinary human relationship, He has an other than merely human ancestry; and once again it ranks with His mother and His brethren those who are willing to do the will of

THE VIRGIN BIRTH

God. But it was precisely this other than ordinary physical motherhood that made Mary what she was. Carefully read in the light of the whole, these sayings only confirm the Gospel story of our Lord's birth and His mother's relationship to Him. Even if it may still be felt that there was sometimes a lack of complete understanding between His mother and Jesus, this need not throw any doubt upon the revelation with which His birth was accompanied; Mary, like John the Baptist, may have preconceived His mission on different lines than those in which Jesus was following in giving Himself to the crowds of poor and needy, instead of making for some position where He could lead His nation out of bondage and assume the power which was His. Since this similar misunderstanding was felt by His Apostles, it would carry no more blame to Mary than it did in their case; and at any rate she was one of the first to understand sufficiently to take her stand by the Cross, faithful in love to Him and fearless of all consequences. Christ's committal of His mother and the beloved disciple one to another is not merely an act by which He commended His mother to the guardianship of the disciple He loved, but it carries with it a mystical and spiritual significance; it is the union of the old dispensation with the new, the carrying over of the Old Testament Church as the inheritance of the Church of the New Testament; and it is a saying which makes Mary the mother of all Christ's loving disciples.

Early ecclesiastical tradition held that Mary remained a virgin and that she had no other children but Jesus. There are, however, references in the Gospels and in the Epistles to the brethren of our Lord; but it seems allowable to think that these were either stepbrothers of our Lord or His cousins; for the Hebrew usage of the word "brethren" is much wider than our own. After the wonderful birth of Jesus, it would surely be natural for Mary to dedicate herself to perpetual virginity. We know Joseph disappears from the story soon afterwards and must have died; and if the brethren of Jesus had been younger they would have been much more likely to accept His leadership, whereas from the Gospel record we learn that at first they did not believe in Him; they have every appearance of being older than He and not His brothers by birth.

Even the admittedly merely poetic representation of the Coronation of Mary in heaven is only another type of representation of that which we find in the Book of Revelation, when our Lord promises to all who overcome a place on His throne; the Coronation of Mary represents the exaltation of our humanity, and particularly of womanhood, which Mary's co-operation with the divine will secured for us; and it is natural to believe that she is granted a supreme exaltation among the saints. It is in her that our humanity is crowned, as it was in her that there began the exaltation of the lowly and the meek. Therefore, although so lowly in herself, having no official position in the Church, and of course infinitely removed from even any approximation to the divine nature of her Son, Mary stands as the "most blessed among women," the first and highest of all the Christian saints, the mother of all Christians, and is even rightly called the "Mother of God," because He who consented to be born of her flesh as true man was also very God.

IX

THE APOSTOLIC CHRISTOLOGY

THE Apostolic Christology is a convenient term under which we may gather together the teaching of the Apostolic writings concerning the person of Christ. But first it must be noted that the Apostolic writings is a term loosely used to cover the whole of the New Testament outside the four Gospels, for it is only a few of these writings that claim to have been written by any of the original Apostles. The authorship of some of them is doubtful, and the authenticity of others is challenged, while far the greater bulk of the epistolary section of the New Testament comes from the hands of one who counted himself an apostle and who was received as such by the original Apostles, and yet who was not a disciple of Christ during His earthly life and probably never saw Jesus in the flesh, namely, St. Paul, the Apostle to the Gentiles. But the question of authorship does not materially affect our present inquiry, which is simply to discover what was the recognized and authoritative conception of Christ held by the Church of the first century. If we had to decide, with the overwhelming majority of critical opinion, that the Epistle to the Hebrews was not written by St. Paul; with radical critics, that the Apocalypse and the Epistles of St. John are by different hands, and neither by the Apostle John; or, with many critics, that the Second Epistle of St. Peter is spurious, we should nevertheless only be increasing the volume of testimony to the unity of opinion in the Early Church concerning the person and place of Jesus Christ.

THE APOSTOLIC CHRISTOLOGY

But before we inquire what exactly these various writings teach concerning Jesus Christ, we must remember the nature of the documents before us, and what, therefore, we may reasonably expect to gather from them. For these documents are in no sense formal theological treatises. They are none of them written to expound or defend the fundamental doctrines accepted by the members of the Church: those doctrines had been previously and otherwise imparted and were taken for granted. Doctrine concerning Christ's person is therefore only to be gathered from expressions used in a salutation or a doxology; where it is made the basis for some exhortation we shall gather what could be assumed; and full and explicit formulation is only to be looked for where controversy has been raised or some error has emerged. Many of the letters were written to meet some crisis; some of them concern personal relations, and the particular subject on which we are seeking for information, namely, what was the doctrine of the Early Church concerning the person of Christ, is one that is given little systematic exposition, just because it was never called into question, and there was no controversy concerning it. We know precisely and unambiguously what was St. Paul's attitude concerning the obligation of Gentile Christians to the ordinances of the Jewish Law, because that was a matter of bitter and widespread dispute. In the very latest Epistles we shall find certain doctrines about the place and person of Jesus Christ insisted upon, because certain questions about these had arisen; but it is interesting to notice exactly what those questions were. From the Epistle to the Colossians we gather that there was a tendency to interpose between Christ and man a number of intermediary beings, consisting of semi-personal powers and angelic hierarchies; while not denying the reality of either, St. Paul declares that Christ is not only higher than all, which was not disputed, but embraces them all, so that there is no need to go to Him through them. Again, from the Epistles of St. John we gather there had been creeping into the Church a curious error which denied that Jesus Christ had come in the flesh : apparently the earliest form of a heresy which was afterwards known as Docetism, which denied, not the reality of Christ's divinity, but the reality of His humanity, regarding the Incarnation as a kind of theophany, and the humanity of Jesus being reduced to a mere disguise or unreal appearance. It will be noted, therefore, that the emergence of the earliest errors, which called for more explicit instruction, were due to Christ being given so high a place that it was felt further mediators were necessary, and to His divinity being held with such emphasis that His humanity was in danger of being refined away. But apart from the controversies which called for definite and detailed statement of doctrine, and remembering that agreed doctrine will mostly only be referred to as assumed, we might, nevertheless, expect to find that the writings of the New Testament would yield sufficient evidence to show what place Jesus Christ was believed to hold in relation both to God and man.

There is nowhere any dispute that while the Gospels present us with the human figure of Jesus as He appeared and spoke to men, the Epistles, while concerned with that same person, both in their devotional expression and doctrinal statement assume for Him a most exalted place in the order of being. It would be a mistake, however, to concern ourselves solely with the place that Jesus Christ is given in the order of being, while neglecting the place that is given to Him in the scheme of salvation. While it was the confident faith of the Old Testa-

THE APOSTOLIC CHRISTOLOGY

ment that salvation was of the Lord, it is the confident assertion of the New Testament that salvation is mediated through the person and work of Jesus Christ. Moreover, the character of the salvation as set forth in the New Testament sufficiently indicates the place that Christ must hold. Salvation from political enemies and social injustice might have been wrought by a Messianic king; the way of salvation from wrong ideas and slavery to sin might have been taught by a specially illuminated prophet; but the salvation set forth in the New Testament is the bringing of men to God, which means not merely to a true knowledge and worship of God, or even to some high form of communion with Him, but to an actual participation in His nature and glory: a salvation which makes men sons of God. This is effected by an intimate personal union between the soul and Christ; but that obviously demands that Christ must Himself first be in intimate personal union with God. It is the salvation wrought by Christ that the Epistles expound; but this rests upon a doctrine concerning Christ which needed no exposition.

It is also undisputed that in the Epistles Christ is so consistently bracketed with God that it seems almost impossible for the writers to mention God without coupling with Him the name of Jesus Christ. And it is more than a placing of God the Father and the Lord Jesus Christ side by side; the names God and Lord are almost interchangeable. The title "Kyrios" (Κύριος), which we translate "Lord," is the common designation of Jesus Christ. This title, like our own "Lord," can be applied to human creatures and to heavenly beings as well as to God, and therefore a certain ambiguity is involved. But Jesus is not only addressed as Lord. His name is hardly ever used without this title being prefixed, and He is often referred to simply as "the Lord." Now, "Kyrios" was used in the Greek translation of the Old Testament as the equivalent of the Hebrew word we pronounce as "Jehovah"; passages where "Lord" is applied to God in the Old Testament are sometimes applied to Christ in the Epistles, and often where "Lord" stands by itself in the New Testament it is difficult to know whether it refers to God or Christ. The significance of the title is therefore a most exalted one, and involves some form of divinity.

But not only is Jesus given the sole mediatorial position in regard to human salvation, He is given a similar position in regard to the creation. Just as salvation comes from God but is ministered through Christ, so creation is referred to God; but Christ is regarded as the agent through whom it was wrought, by whom it is maintained, and towards whom as goal it moves. This claim ranks Christ above creatures; He is regarded not only as having existed before He entered this life, but He existed before all creation, and the creation actually came into being through Him. There could be no greater distinction in Hebrew religion than that between the creature and the Creator; the New Testament maintains that distinction with solemn emphasis, and if these are the only two divisions of being, then Christ does not belong to the created but to the creative side. What then is His relation to God the Father and the Creator? This is set forth in various terms and images: He is "the Son of God"; He is "the image of the invisible God"; He existed originally in the "form of God"; He is "the expression of God's essence," "the outshining of His glory." Again, He is "on the right hand of God" and "in the glory of the Father"; and "in Him dwelleth all the fulness of the Godhead bodily."

THE APOSTOLIC CHRISTOLOGY

But, as is well known and easily realized these explanations and titles only raise inevitable questions for those who believe that there is only one God and that God is one ; and it is difficult to believe that these questions did not emerge for all the New Testament writers, trained as they were in a passionate adherence to monotheism, and with an abhorrence of any infringement of the sole majesty of God, or the offering of worship to a mere creature; especially as they constantly and explicitly maintain the monotheistic creed of Hebrew religion. How then could these writers give so high a place to Christ without defining whether, or in what sense, He was divine, and how this affected the unity of the Godhead ? Yet this is just what they neither define nor discuss. This ambiguous and anomalous position given to Christ in the New Testament writings has been explained by supposing that an unconscious and unconsidered growth has taken place, conditioned by religious experience, the fervour of devotion, and the adoption of theological notions derived from other sources. St. Paul has often been charged with being the chief agent in this development, by whose influence the very Gospel has entirely changed its character ; and so there was bequeathed to the Church a complicated and contradictory system, which ecclesiastical doctrine could only straighten out and make intelligible by carrying the process further and ascribing deity to Christ, that being made possible by defining the Godhead as triune. Sometimes this growth is regarded as a gradual corruption of a beautifully simple and sufficient faith, and sometimes as the inevitable explanation of what was already implied in the Gospels or necessitated by the irrepressible devotion which Christ, by the religious experience He generated, called out. But before we decide which of

THE APOSTOLIC CHRISTOLOGY

these explanations is true, we have to ask if it is true that the New Testament reveals a growth in its estimate concerning Jesus Christ. Now it is difficult to answer the question whether there has been growth by a plain yes or no. To read St. Mark's Gospel and then, say, the Epistle to the Colossians, and not to be aware of a difference both in thought and terminology would be impossible. On the other hand, growth might be by a mere addition, like a building; a natural development, as the full-grown oak develops from the acorn; by explicit evolution of what was implicitly involved, thus developing logical clearness and richness of thought.

It is possible to arrange our New Testament writings in an order which emphasizes the change that has taken place, and would correspond roughly to their chronological sequence. There would come first those which preserve a primitive flavour and retain a Jewish terminology, and in this group we place the early speeches in the Acts of the Apostles, the Epistle of St. James, the two Epistles of St. Peter, and the Epistle of St. Jude. In the second group come the Pauline Epistles with their definite characteristics. In the third group we can place the Epistle to the Hebrews, for, even in the unlikely possibility of its being St. Paul's, it marks a distinct type of thought. In the fourth group we can place all the Johannine writings. Now it will be admitted that the speeches of St. Peter in the Acts are unadvanced in the terminology they apply to Jesus. Jesus, in them, is referred to as a man approved of God, and anointed with the Holy Ghost; He is called His servant Jesus, whom God glorified; one made both Lord and Christ, exalted to be a prince and a saviour, and now at the right hand of God. But it must be remembered that these speeches were addressed to a Jewish audience and naturally began with the facts they accepted, and used language they could understand and most easily adopt. It is the Messiahship of Jesus that St. Peter is here seeking to set forth and get accepted. But we can find speeches by St. Paul in the Acts where the Christology is not only at the same stage, but where there is hardly any Christology at all; for instance, when St. Paul was speaking to the superstitious populace at Lystra or the philosophical audience at Athens he endeavoured to place himself on the religious level of the people to whom he was speaking, though he had no intention of leaving them there. Moreover, the Messianic terminology of St. Peter in these early speeches is exalted and certainly involves more than merely Messianic functions, while in addition we have such expressions as the Prince of life, Lord of all, and Judge of the living and the dead applied to Jesus, which, without being definitely theological, obviously demand some theological justification. We can group with these early speeches the Epistles of St. James, of St. Peter, and St. Jude. It must be admitted that the Epistle of St. James is meagre in Christological doctrine and even in distinctive Christian reference. The Epistle was, however, written to the Jews of the Dispersion and may have had a conciliatory purpose; nevertheless, Jesus Christ is placed alongside God in the opening salutation; He is called " the Lord of glory," and while God is called " the Lord and Father," Jesus is also indisputably called simply " the Lord " without any further identification. The lordship of Jesus is therefore assumed as beyond dispute, and spoken of in the same way as the lordship of God. The first Epistle of St. Peter contains no special Christological doctrine, but the bracketing of the Lord Jesus Christ alongside the Father, the application of the title Lord equally to God and Christ, and the use of the term in the exhortation

THE APOSTOLIC CHRISTOLOGY

"sanctify Christ as Lord in your hearts" shows that it is no mere title of respect, but a description of Christ's place and power. In the Epistle of St. Jude, Jesus is not only called "the Lord," but the *Despotes*, a word which is elsewhere used for God conceived as the mighty Creator.

When we pass from this group to the Pauline Epistles we certainly find much more Christological material; but is there any indication that this material is the exclusive invention of the Apostle Paul? In the main this material is employed in explicating the significance of the title "Lord" given to Jesus, working out in a more detailed fashion His mediatorial position in the work of our salvation, and setting forth the relationship to the Father implied in the constant coupling of their names. Before we can decide whether St. Paul has added anything to the generally accepted doctrine we must take notice of the further suggestion that the apostle's own doctrine has undergone a development. To decide this question we may take the high position given to Jesus Christ in the later Epistles and see whether this involves anything new. In the Colossians Christ's agency in the creation is emphasized and all the fulness of the Godhead is said to dwell in Him bodily. But we can find all this expressed, though in briefer form, in the First Epistle to the Corinthians, "There is one God the Father, of whom are all things . . . and one Lord, Jesus Christ, through whom are all things," and in the Second Epistle to the Corinthians God is said to have been "in Christ reconciling the world unto Himself." And when in the Epistle to the Ephesians this reconciling work is further expounded, it only details its universal reference. It is in the Epistle to the Philippians that the Christology of the apostle is most fully set forth, but even there it is only used to set forth Christ's renunciation in coming to this world as an example of humility; and the whole passage is only an expansion of the shorter statement in II Corinthians, " though He was rich, yet for your sakes He became poor." Nowhere is there any indication that St. Paul is bringing forward a new doctrine; it is assumed to be accepted by his readers. Now, the apostle had demanded that the Gentiles should be admitted to the Church without submitting to the observances of the Jewish Law, and this had created acute controversy throughout the Churches; and St. Paul had had to defend himself against persecution and misrepresentation over this issue; but never do his traducers affirm that he has brought in novel doctrine about Christ, which their hostility and Jewish prejudice would have been quick to detect.

The Epistle to the Hebrews, which stands in a class apart, and emphasizes the humanity of Christ, nevertheless contains a very high Christology, inasmuch as it also refers to Christ's agency in the creation and sustaining of the world, makes His character the expression of God's Person and applies the Old Testament words " Thy throne, O God, is for ever " directly to Christ.

In the fourth section we place the Johannine writings. The Christology of the Apocalypse is symbolic, but not only uses the same language of Christ as of God, and yields Him divine worship, but makes the Lamb the only *visible* object of worship. The Epistles insist that our knowledge of God is dependent upon our faith in the Incarnate Son. But in this section we must include the Prologue to the Fourth Gospel, which gives to Christ the ascription of absolute Divinity and expresses His relationship to God as that of His Word and brings Him near to man by means of the Incarnation. In this Prologue

THE APOSTOLIC CHRISTOLOGY

the evangelist identifies Christ with the pre-existing Word (*Logos*) and declares that the Logos existed before all things, was the cause of their creation, was eternally with God, and was divine. It has been supposed that the evangelist has had recourse to Greek philosophy in order to explain the relationship of Christ to God, and that here is a clear instance of drawing from alien sources, which has led to the complication of the simpler faith and to the exaggerated position given to Christ. But the Johannine emphasis upon Christ's place in the creation agrees with the testimony of St. Paul and the Epistle to the Hebrews. It is unlikely that it has been arrived at through the influence of either of these writers. Each of them approaches this doctrine by a different route; neither St. Paul nor the writer to the Hebrews mentions the Logos; moreover it is very questionable if the source of the Logos doctrine in St. John has anything to do with Greek philosophy. If we turn to the Apocalypse we shall find that there also Christ is called "the Word of God," and in the First Epistle of St. John we get the reference "that which we have heard ... concerning the Word of life." In neither of these cases would it have occurred to anyone to seek in Greek philosophy the origin of "the Word"; and when the author of the Hebrews speaks of Christ "upholding all things by the word of His power" he uses a different expression for "word," namely *rhema*, as if he studiously avoided *Logos*.

It may be admitted that in all this we can discern a growth in the widening and deepening thought concerning the significance of Christ, but nowhere can we detect the bringing in of new doctrine by which one who was originally regarded simply as a human teacher is gradually invested with the Divine Essence. And here we can take note of the fact that

THE APOSTOLIC CHRISTOLOGY

some scholars have denied that Christ is ever directly and indisputably called God in the New Testament. It is this latter point which we have now to investigate. There are only a few passages in dispute.

St. Paul, in speaking of Christ, when writing to the Romans, goes on to exclaim " who is over all, God blessed for ever." The question is whether this is a doxology into which the Apostle Paul suddenly bursts, or whether these words are an ascription to Christ of undoubtedly divine honours. If we are to decide solely by syntax and grammar it is the latter explanation which must rule. It is held, however, to be so unparalleled for Christ to be called God that many scholars prefer the former alternative. Again, in the Epistle to Titus we have a text which may be translated either " the appearing of the glory of the great God and of our Saviour Jesus Christ " or " the appearing of the glory of our great God and Saviour Jesus Christ." Here grammar and the natural reference seem on the side of the latter alternative, yet it is also possible to take this to be a double reference first to God and secondly to Christ. It is interesting in this connection to note that in the Pastoral Epistles God is more than once called the Saviour, while that same expression is still applied to Christ; which makes another reference in Titus to " God our Saviour " also ambiguous. But for our present purpose it is unnecessary to use any of these passages as an argument for the divinity of Christ, and we can afford to allow that nowhere in the New Testament is Christ called simply and explicitly God; for even in the Epistle to the Hebrews the quotation from the Old Testament, " thy throne, O God, is for ever and ever," undoubtedly applied to Christ, need carry no more than the quotation itself implies in an Old Testament passage, where the word can sometimes be used in a sense that does not denote absolute divinity;

THE APOSTOLIC CHRISTOLOGY

and while there can be no doubt concerning the divinity ascribed to the Logos in the Fourth Gospel, it might still be argued that it was only indirectly ascribed to Christ, or only applied divinity in a secondary sense; though it is difficult to explain away St. Thomas's exclamation " my Lord and my God." But we are willing to concede, for the sake of argument, that never in the New Testament is the word God unequivocally, and beyond all dispute, directly applied to Christ. Indeed, we can give the fullest weight possible, not only to this fact, but to another, namely that there are a number of passages which seem purposely to differentiate Christ from God, while there are other passages which have been taken to involve the denial to Him of actual divinity. These must now be briefly examined.

The New Testament affirms more than once, and always assumes, that there is only one God. St. Paul seems to declare that this one God is the Father: " there is one God, the Father," though this depends upon the punctuation. In the Epistle to Timothy we read " there is one God, one mediator also between God and men, a man Christ Jesus "; this is the literal translation, though it probably means " himself man "; at any rate it is the humanity of Christ that is insisted on. Again in the Epistle to the Romans we have the doxology, " to the only wise God, through Jesus Christ "; and again in St. Jude, " to the only God our Saviour, through Jesus Christ our Lord." Moreover, it is common to speak of " the God and Father of our Lord Jesus Christ," and although grammatically this might mean the God who is also the Father of our Lord Jesus Christ, we have a passage in the Ephesians which reads simply " the God of our Lord Jesus Christ." It might be argued that if the Father is the God

THE APOSTOLIC CHRISTOLOGY

of Jesus Christ, He Himself cannot be God. But if we were to take these texts as denials that Christ was divine, then we should have to decide what else He could be, for His name is constantly placed alongside the name of God, and apparently on an equal level in such connections as " the grace of the Lord Jesus Christ, and the love of God, and the fellowship of the Holy Ghost " ; " the same Spirit . . . the same Lord . . . the same God " ; " one Spirit . . . one Lord . . . one God and Father " ; so that we are bound to ask who is this that is placed in such proximity to God, and yet apparently is not God ? Can we conceive that the New Testament writers had never thought the matter out ; or had allowed their devotion to exalt Jesus Christ to the highest possible place, while their monotheistic training restrained them from a definite ascription of Godhead ; or that they had seized upon the distinction between Lord and God in order to evade the difficulty ? If we are unwilling to consider such an impossible hypothesis, then we are compelled to have recourse to the later formulated theology of the Church to find any explanation. Then the solution is simple :

It is that in the New Testament Jesus Christ, while placed alongside God, and invested with Divine attributes, is never, or very rarely called God, for the reason that He was not simply God, but God made man, God and man ; so that to apply to Christ the word God without qualification would lead to error and confusion, as it still often does. It may be felt, however, that this solution is too simple, especially since Christ is never called by such titles as " the God-man " or " God and man " or " God become man " ; and yet, as we shall see, when we come to examine the Christ of the Creeds, no other solution of the New Testament faith is possible. The only point

THE APOSTOLIC CHRISTOLOGY

that has to be determined is whether in the Apostolic Church, the faith was held in an inchoate form, of which the later ecclesiastical doctrine is the only possible formulation; or whether, though not of course in the terms of the later doctrine, but in thought and substance, Christ was held to be truly God and really man. If these alternatives are the only ones open, the modern mind will be more attracted to the former, and the Church's doctrine will then be regarded as an inevitable, logical deduction from of the New Testament Christology, simply making clearer and more defiinte what was held in a less formal and explicit fashion. But it needs to be pointed out that if this solution is chosen, it is a solution that involves an entirely supernatural inspiration, for it means that thought moved on independent lines converging infallibly towards an unforseen goal. It would be simpler to hold that the Apostles and the Church as a whole had a much more clearly defined Christology than is generally understood, not yet fixed in language, but perfectly clear in thought, so that it could be not only assumed as accepted and great exhortations based upon it, but appealed to in order to resist the invasion of error. The terminology used to express this common faith was in the main derived from Old Testament Scripture, but its meaning was clear, and its choice must have been deliberate.

To sum up, therefore, Jesus was called Lord, first because this was a recognized divine title; next, because it distinguished Jesus from the word God when used for the Godhead or the Father; but especially because it had been used for Jehovah and so could stand for God as personally revealed, thus identifying Jesus with God as revealed to man, not only in salvation, but in the creation of the visible world; and this distinction is eternal, which the

THE APOSTOLIC CHRISTOLOGY

Apocalypse teaches in symbolic fashion by setting forth the Lamb upon the throne as the only visible form of God.

According to the Apostolic Christology, therefore, Jesus Christ is God as revealed, God as incarnate; truly divine, but having stripped Himself of outward signs of divinity to live a human life and win exaltation back again by His Father's gift and man's confession; although He was the eternal Son of God learning through a human experience interior sympathy with our condition so that He might unite mankind to Himself and lift us to a share in His Divine Sonship; receiving from the Father all authority in heaven and earth, until He shall have gained the grateful and adoring submission of the creatures He has redeemed and reconciled, and then submitting Himself, with those He has united to Himself, unto the Father, neither Christ nor they absorbed or reduced to a subordinate place, but embraced in the unity of the Godhead, that God may be all in all.

X

THE CHRIST OF THE CREEDS

IT would be a most indiscriminating mind which perceived no difference when it passed from the Gospel portrait of Jesus to the Christological paragraphs of the Athanasian Creed; but it would be an impatient mind which concluded that the person referred to in the different documents was not the same; and an unconsidering mind that dismissed the latter document as an unnecessary complication of the simplicity of Christ, an obscuration of His vital personality beneath lifeless abstractions. Yet such, it is to be feared, is the judgment to which the modern mind often hurries, and to which even the Christian sentiment of our generation is often tempted. This tendency is not due merely to a failure to estimate the difference between the purpose of the Gospel and the purposes of the Creed; for if so, it would be sufficient to point out that the Creed presupposes the Gospel portrait as referred to, and assumes that the living person there portrayed is known through interior experience. It hardly meets the situation to call attention to the essential difference between a flower growing in its natural surroundings and when dried and pressed in a herbarium; for it is a marked tendency of the modern mind to believe that the intellect only devitalizes what it touches, and definition only destroys the power of appreciation. But it is at least remarkable that the Christian Church, and in particular Catholic theology, should stand for the rights of the intellect and the need

THE CHRIST OF THE CREEDS

for scientific definition, while still determined to keep the intellect in its place, and admitting that definition is not the same thing as experience. And herein it appeals not only to a more balanced view of things, to which our generation, with its passion for vitality and yet its love for vagueness, has yet to attain, but it is in line with common facts and common sense; for although it might be thought that the flower could be identified just as easily without knowing its name, and its beauty enjoyed just as much without knowing how to dissect it, this is actually not the case. Until the flower has had its identity labelled by a name, which distinguishes as well as classifies it, it is not so easily recognized when it is met again. And a person with any sense of beauty will only increase appreciation by having attention drawn to the beauty of its separate parts and its functional provision.

Doctrinal orthodoxy may sometimes be made a substitute for devotional fervour and mystical experience, but that is not the fault of doctrinal orthodoxy, but of man's deceptive nature; while it can be shown that the departure from doctrinal orthodoxy eventually withers up devotion and leads mystical experience into the clouds or into the desert. This may suffice to induce at least patience with the Church's attempt to find an explanation of the person of Christ which shall not only satisfy the mind, but by that very means deepen devotion and make its application to character and life all the more certain and far-reaching. It is admitted that the Creeds cannot do without the Gospel, and that they are useless without personal appropriation, but the Church has never presented the one alone, or as a substitute for the others, but all three together.

THE CHRIST OF THE CREEDS

It may be shown that the Gospel needed the protection of the Creeds, for in defence of the general necessity for conciliar definitions and the drawing up of the Creeds it can be urged that this was not a task undertaken merely to satisfy intellectual curiosity or scientific interest, but the Church was compelled to take this action, not only because inadequate statements concerning Christ were being made which, if adopted, would have destroyed the assurance of revelation and the hope of redemption, but these statements were leading to controversies which were dividing the Church and making fellowship impossible. For although statements can often be found in honoured teachers of the Church which, from the point of view of later definitions, are inadequate, confused, or even unorthodox; they were either not made definitively, the terms employed had not gathered the later meaning which controversy developed, or they had not been the cause of disturbance and dissension. It may be stated as extremely likely that if heresies had never arisen the Church would not have drawn up any creeds at all. And yet we ought not to regret that heresies arose which made this necessary, for the definitions of the Creeds have saved Christianity from being swamped with alien thought and dissipated into vague generalities.

But even if sympathy can be gained for the necessity of creeds in general, the objection is then often raised that the discussions are so hairsplitting and the definitions expressed in such abstract and philosophical terminology. But in matters of vital importance hairsplitting is often necessary, for the slightest deviation from the truth may produce something more dangerous, because more specious, than downright contradiction and a flagrant lie. The terms chosen do not really commit the Church to partisan philosophies, as is sometimes alleged, but are terms which carry a sufficiently agreed connotation in all regions of thought; and it ought to be welcomed as a tolerant action for the Church to be willing to take the considered thought of the human mind, even outside its own fold, as in itself holding truth, and as able to bring valuable contribution to the elucidation of the faith.

But then it is often objected that the way in which the definitions of the Church are dogmatically laid down limits further discussion and paralyses progress. This is to misunderstand the meaning of dogma. A dogma is, after all, only an authoritative decision that on certain issues that have been raised the truth lies on this side rather than on that, that a certain term best guards the truth, or that a certain assumption is necessary if the truth is to be reached. It is quite possible, and even necessary, for those who do not believe that the Church has not been divinely guided to go behind these decisions and reopen the whole matter; but it will generally be found that such inquiries establish respect for the Church's decisions on the issues in question, and it has been proved to be a waste of time to be continually going behind these decisions. Moreover, it can be shown that these decisions only open the road for further discussion, whereas a decision in the opposite direction would have made further discussion impossible. It is the heresies which lead into a cul-de-sac; the dogmas are starting-points and sign-posts along the open road. This is a matter on which men must persuade themselves by patient discovery, but it need not be feared that impartial inquiry will do anything save show that the Church was divinely guided in these critical issues of faith.

But even if men can be persuaded of this, they

are often perplexed and made suspicious by the temper in which ecclesiastical discussions were carried on, the personal animosities, the wire-pulling and the violence by which decisions were obtained and their acceptance exacted. But it may be taken as a general rule that when men quarrel violently it is over something that matters, and an easy, widespread tolerance often goes only with the acceptance of formulæ which are so comprehensive as to be meaningless. It may be admitted that personalities often entered in, and that impatience and harshness often characterized the victorious party; but the divine purpose has to work through human instruments which are often stained and bent, yet the purpose is achieved despite these imperfections. And if the history of the early controversies concerning the person of Christ is patiently and sympathetically studied with the desire to find the truth on this subject, it will be found that at any rate the violence was not all on the orthodox side. It has sometimes been stated that the findings of the Nicene Council were only adopted because the Emperor desired them, and accepted because they came with the force of an Imperial decree. But this is completely untrue. The Emperor certainly wanted a decision, for the sake of peace, but, like others since, he thought the quarrel was over a quibble; and, as his action afterwards proved, his own leanings were towards Arianism; and so far from the findings of the Council being unthinkingly accepted by the Church as a whole, the leader of the Nicene party spent most of his life in banishment, and half a century afterwards the opposition was so powerful that, in the memorable phrase of Jerome, "the whole world groaned, astonished to find itself Arian." It was only by the superior theological abilities of the Cappadocian theologians, Basil and the two Gregorys, and the persuasive powers of men like Hilary, that the Nicene formula was at length accepted by the whole Church.

Once the recognition of this position has been gained, it is possible to go on to point out that it was more than a passion for dialectical subtlety or the determination to force definitions on rebels that was at work. It was absolutely necessary to defend the devotion given to Jesus Christ against any charge of idolatry and so to define His place as to maintain a purely monotheistic faith. This was the real issue behind the Nicene controversy: if Jesus was not truly God, then the Church's worship of Him was a relapse into paganism. And although, when it was decided that Christ was of the "same substance with the Father," and therefore worthy to be worshipped with the Father, this only provoked the ensuing controversy as to the relation of the humanity of Christ to His divinity, this was neither a case of complication breeding complication, nor of the faith being forgotten and lost in dialectical discussion; for what lay behind the new issue, finally settled at Chalcedon, was whether God had become man in such a way as to give promise of the redemption of our whole humanity. The issue at Nicea was the certainty of revelation; the issue at Chalcedon the certainty of redemption; in both cases the issue was simply and solely religious.

With this preliminary plea for a patient investigation we must now content ourselves with showing how the various heresies swung from one extreme to another; how the Church chose either the middle way between extremes, or the comprehension of complementary truth, until, almost by mathematical precision, the heresies exhausted

THE CHRIST OF THE CREEDS

all possible alternatives, and indicated the only position which would be a safeguard against the error into which they fell, and the only satisfaction of the truth they were trying to state. For in this question it must be remembered that a heresy is not necessarily false in itself, or entirely false; it may be a statement of the truth, but without its complementary balance of other truth; it may be a mere exaggeration, or simply be confused in its language. For instance: according to the Church's faith it is true to say that Christ was God, and yet if this were maintained to be the whole truth about Christ it would be most heretical; just as it is sometimes thought to be heresy to say that Christ was man, whereas this is perfectly true, but it is not the whole truth; for Christ is both God and man. If this is borne in mind; if it is also remembered that at one time a word like the famous *homoousion*, afterwards adopted at Nicea, was previously rejected, but as then used with an unorthodox meaning; and if the charge sometimes made in recent times that the Church, after all, only eventually adopted something very like the heresy it once condemned is countered by demanding discrimination of the actual difference between the two decisions, and by drawing attention to this as a determination to take the truth wherever it was to be found, then the course of this tortuous history becomes plain, the discussions are invested with a new significance, and the result is seen to have a comprehension, a simplicity, a finality and even a beauty that can hardly be exaggerated.

We can now proceed to set forth in the briefest possible way, and in quite general fashion, the emergence of certain conceptions of the person of Christ which the Church condemned as heresy,

THE CHRIST OF THE CREEDS

and the conclusions to which the Church came, through free if fierce discussion, at first openly and then in Councils, which from their composition have generally been recognized as Ecumenical. Save for a reference here and there, we shall not concern ourselves with the details of the discussion, with the persons concerned, or even with the exact chronological order, but only with the general movement of thought, the opinions condemned and the conclusions finally reached.

Amongst the first of the heresies to be condemned was that known as *Ebionism*, probably so called from the Hebrew word *Ebion*, " poor," and perhaps therefore professed by Jewish Christians, who for various reasons were predominantly poor, or by an Essene sect who had embraced poverty. This heresy regarded Christ as a mere man and nothing more, though, of course, specially endowed with grace and filled with the Spirit. Some students of dogmatic history have been inclined to believe that this was the original faith of the Early Church, which was added to, and transformed out of all recognition, first by the Apostle Paul, then by the Johannine writings, and finally by the theologians of the post-Nicene period. But there is no historical evidence for this, and everything is against it. The heresy was never widespread, it was never professed by any great leader or theologian in the Church, and seems to have been rather the opinion of small Jewish sects who had moved as far as recognizing Christ as the Messiah, but no farther, and never had any real part or influence in the Church's life. This estimate of its original position is confirmed by the fact that at the same time, and probably even earlier, there arose the entirely opposite heresy known as *Docetism*, which held that Christ was

THE CHRIST OF THE CREEDS

never a man at all, but only a divine being masquerading under a human disguise. This, however, was also never an opinion widely represented in the Church, but seems to have been put forward mainly by Gnostic sects, whose principles compelled this conclusion, because they held anything material, and especially human flesh, to be essentially evil, with which the Divine could have no contact. The beginnings of this conception seem traceable as far back as New Testament times, for it seems to be combated in the First Epistle of St. John. But these two extremes were obviously too crude to gain any acceptance where the Apostolic theology or the Gospel portrait of Christ was kept in mind; nevertheless, they begin to mark out the extremes towards which thought was inclined to swing, first on one side and then on the other.

Therefore the next heresies which emerge are those which attempt to state these positions in a less extreme form; and so we get *Adoptionism*, that is, the theory that Christ was only a man, but for His merits was elevated to divine rank. This savoured too much of the deifications to which paganism was prone; and although it was fathered by men of much greater weight, and has not been without attraction for the modern mind, it involves impossible theological conceptions; for, after all, it is only an " apotheosis of a Godman, not an incarnation of God." At the other extreme appeared a further refinement of the Docetic heresy known as *Cerinthianism*, from the founder Cerinthus, who taught that a divine emanation descended upon Jesus at His baptism, but left Him just before the Crucifixion. Its crudity only appealed to the Gnostic sects, and never had any kind of welcome in the historic Church. These two extremes now draw nearer

THE CHRIST OF THE CREEDS

together in the first great theological controversy of the Church, raised by Arius, and named after him *Arianism*. This heresy, refusing to Christ a place within the Godhead, and yet recognizing that he was not a mere man, attempted to solve the problem by regarding Him as a created being lower than God, but higher than man. And this again approximated, on the one hand to the pagan conception of a demi-god, and on the other to the Docetic and Gnostic denials of Christ's humanity. Such a conception, which has been not unfairly described as " the incarnation of that which was not God in that which was not man," could hardly be expected to win assent, and it would never have been such a danger to the Church but for the recent influx of semi-Christianized pagans, the extraordinary energy of its leaders, the political power it was able to obtain, and the difficulty of agreeing upon a formula that would absolutely exclude its taint and tendency.

To settle this controversy the First General Council of the Church was called, met at Nicea and accepted the declaration that Christ was of the *" same substance* with the Father," adopting the Greek word *homoousion*, which has thus become one of the most famous and best known terms in Christian theology. This defined the nature of Christ as absolutely divine, that is, of the same nature as God. The term was unscriptural; it had been used by heretics, and had actually been condemned by a Synod of the Church; although in both those cases it was employed for a different purpose and with a different meaning. And it took sixty years of strife and controversy to make it perfectly clear what was meant by this phrase, and to get it willingly accepted by the Church as a whole, as the only adequate safeguard of the truth.

But now that the divinity of Christ had been decided upon in so clear and absolute a fashion, the question was immediately forced to the front as to how, then, Christ's humanity was related to His divinity; and a theory was now put forward by Apollinaris which attempted to solve this question by maintaining that the place of the rational soul, or the mind, as we should call it, was taken in Christ by the Logos. Apollinaris thought this was necessary because it was the mind in man that was the centre of sin, and this had to be displaced by something wholly divine. But as it was soon pointed out, this did not redeem that portion of our humanity that was in most need of it, but simply got rid of it; for " what was not assumed was not redeemed." While the earlier heresies had made Christ wholly God or wholly man, Arianism had made Him neither God nor man, and *Apollinarianism* now made Him half God and half man. And yet it must be noted that this heresy was beginning to mark the way to the only possible solution.

But in order to swing away from this danger, an attempt was made at the opposite extreme; and the heresy called *Nestorianism* stands for the view that there are two complete personalities in Christ, the divine eternal personality of the Logos and the human personality born of Mary. It was the determination to preserve this distinction that made it impossible for Nestorius to accept the definition of Mary as the *Theotokos*, namely, the bearer of God. It is questionable whether Nestorius ever really held the view that there were two persons in Christ, and it may have been that he himself was never in the strict sense of the word a heretic at all, and that an injustice was done to him on this score. Further evidence of his opinions seems to show that he held that there were two separate personalities, but that they became one, only it would seem that this union was conceived as a mere contact between persons and not a real unity, and is, therefore, no basis for either the Incarnation or the Atonement. At any rate, the opinions which were condemned as Nestorianism are obviously impossible, though they also have been looked at favourably in modern times, under the idea that unless there was born of Mary a new personality, there is no other way of securing for Christ a full and true humanity. But these opinions, old or new, leave the impression that God was in Christ only by a species of indwelling or communion: there is no true Incarnation.

The opposition to this rejected dualism in Christ's personality then tempted men to venture to the opposite extreme, and to declare that there was not only but one person in Christ, there was but one nature. This was known as *Eutychianism* from the person who proclaimed it, or as *Monophysitism* from the opinion that it put forward. Cyril, the great opponent of Nestorius, had used the phrase "one nature," though by it he probably meant the one nature of the divine person who became flesh, and so assumed another nature. But some of Cyril's followers adopted this phrase incautiously, and maintained that, although Christ came "*of* two natures," after the Incarnation there was only one nature, for the human nature was absorbed into the divine. This again the Church rejected, as it did also its further refinement that if Christ had two natures, He at least had only one will; demanding instead that the humanity of Christ must be complete, including not only real flesh but the rational soul with all its powers. Hence the final definition arrived at at the Council

THE CHRIST OF THE CREEDS

of Chalcedon was that Christ is *one person in two natures*. The decisions of this Council are known to most of us through some of its terminology, being embodied in the Christological articles of the Athanasian Creed: "our Lord Jesus Christ, the Son of God, is God and Man; God of the Substance of the Father, begotten before the worlds: and Man of the Substance of His Mother, born in the world; perfect God and perfect Man: of a reasonable soul and human flesh subsisting; equal to the Father, as touching His Godhead; and inferior to the Father, as touching His Manhood. Who although He be God and Man: yet He is not two, but one Christ." The Council used, however, some other terms which the Athanasian Creed does not contain, but which are so important that they ought to be as widely known: "of the same Substance with the Father concerning His Divinity, and of the same Substance with us concerning His Humanity . . . one and the same Christ . . . in two natures, unconfused, unalterable, indivisible and indissoluble." Under this definition the extremes into which the heresies had fallen are shut out; the truth for which they contended is gathered together; not by way of compromise, nor as a mere *via media* between the two, but by comprehension; the Church, it should be noted, contending as strongly for Christ's humanity as for His divinity.

But the question is bound to be raised, especially in modern times, as to whether this conclusion is true to the Gospel portrait, intelligible to the modern mind, adequate in the light of modern thought and knowledge, and still sufficiently sets forth the nature of Christ's personality so as to guard us from error, and give us an assurance that in Christ God has both revealed Himself to us and redeemed us. The

THE CHRIST OF THE CREEDS

objections that are sometimes raised against the Church's definitions are, first, that the phrase *homoousion* is materialistic, is too metaphysical, or is meaningless. It is an unfortunate thing that the Latin translation of *homoousion* is *substantia*, and the English of that *substance*; for this conveys to many minds something quite physical or material. It need not do so; and since we have no other word, such as essence, nature, or the like, which is much better, we must simply remind ourselves that there can be a purely spiritual as well as a physical substance, and that in regard to God only the former can possibly be intended. Secondly, it has to be pointed out that *homoousion* means not merely that Christ is of the same order of being as God, for this might mean, where monotheism was not strictly held, that there could be two Gods of the same nature, just as there could be two men having the same nature; but it was precisely this that was excluded when the proposal of *homoiousion*, or "like nature," was rejected. In the Nicene Creed *homoousion* is meant to exclude identity of personality while affirming identity of nature; or, more strictly, that Christ is one *being* with the Father, while differentiated in *person* from the Father. The Chalcedonian definition of "one person in two natures" has raised the objection that a human nature that is impersonal would be no human nature at all; but the objection was answered by early defenders of the Chalcedonian formula, and is adequately met, by declaring that the humanity of Christ neither had a personality of its own, nor was it impersonal, but it was *enhypostatic*, which means that its personal subject was the Logos, the eternal Son of God. The idea that the only person in Christ is the Second Person of the Blessed Trinity first of all assures us that

THE CHRIST OF THE CREEDS

we have a direct and immediate revelation of God; secondly, it also shows us how closely the divine and the human are related, in that a divine person can take the place of the human ego, and produce as a result a thoroughly unified being. Moreover, it is perhaps the one convincing proof given to us that God is personal in the sense that we understand the word from our own personality, and therefore can answer to and understand us. Again, objection has been raised to the doctrine of the two natures, since whatever Christ is, He is a unity. But if we are going to deny that there are two natures, we shall be in danger of saying Christ was either only human or only divine, and the Church is defending the most sacred rights of humanity in maintaining that the humanity in Christ was neither absorbed nor destroyed; for this gives us an assurance that we have not to escape our humanity in order to realize our redemption. There is surely some distinction between divine and human nature, and we must therefore maintain the two natures if we are still going to maintain that Christ was both human and divine. And that two natures are seen in operation in the Gospels is evident from the fact that so many of the critics would like to cut out the one side or the other, because it does not agree with their preconceived notions of what is either possible to humanity or demanded by divinity: the one regards His miracles as impossible and the other regards a real human experience as impossible.

If the Church's doctrine of Christ gives us a complicated psychology, it is at least not more complicated than that of man himself; and if we do not complain of the volumes that have to be written to explain human psychology, we can hardly complain of the language of the, after all, much simpler statement that sets forth His dual nature and yet declares for His undivided personality. There is nothing in the Creeds or the Church's definitions which prevents our explaining the terms they used in modern language; indeed, that is always imperative. There is nothing to prevent the Church in a future Ecumenical Council deciding that further explanations are necessary, or clearer terms can now be used. But what any Church that is faithful to past guidance must resist is a denial and contradiction of its decisions; for it knows full well that, however inadequate those terms may be, and all terms will always be in some degree inadequate to the divine mysteries, it is, as Athanasius said at Nicea, " fighting for our all ": for the assurance that God Himself has actually spoken to us, that He has lived within this realm of human experience, and therefore that our humanity is redeemable. But the terminology used by the Creeds is still wide enough for ample discussion, for unfettered progress, and for the fullest application to man's growing personal and social needs. If we only remember that the person set forth in the Creeds is identical with the person portrayed in the Gospels, needing to be known both by the heart and mind, we shall find the Creeds not only necessary and adequate, but a constant inspiration to the redemption of the human body, the education of the human mind and the salvation of human society.

XI
THE DOCTRINE OF THE TRINITY

THE doctrine of the Trinity is the crown and consummation of Christian theology; it constitutes the peculiarly Christian conception of the Godhead, necessitated by the revelation of the divinity of Christ and, the separate personality of the Holy Ghost. It should therefore be the glory of the Christian faith, the chief point in which it surpasses other conceptions of God, and a proof of the supremacy, absoluteness and finality of Christianity. It must be admitted, however, that this is not how the doctrine appeals to many. There are some who feel that it is just at this demand for the acceptance of the Trinitarian conception of God that Christianity proposes something impossible to the human intellect, since to confess that God is at the same time One and Three involves believing that a sheer contradiction can be true. Some who claim to be, and wish to be, regarded as Christians look upon the doctrine as a definite corruption of the religion of Christ and an illegitimate complication of the simple faith of the New Testament, traceable to the influence either of heathen polytheism or of pagan philosophical speculation. Some whose adherence to traditional Christianity would make them shrink from denying a doctrine so embodied in Christian creeds, prayers and hymns, nevertheless regard the completely formulated doctrine as it is expressed, for instance, in the first part of the Athanasian Creed, as an example of speculation having over-

THE DOCTRINE OF THE TRINITY

reached itself, and abstract notions being preferred to the more vital conceptions of faith. There are perhaps even more who, while believing that the Church was compelled to formulate the doctrine at least to the stage contained in the Athanasian Creed, yet feel it to be somewhat of a burden to the intellect, from which they can only find relief by regarding the doctrine as a mystery ultimately incomprehensible to the mind, and to be received merely on authority; and, therefore, they are inclined to relegate it to the background when they are seeking to recommend Christianity to others, or when they are trying to think it out for themselves, while the doctrine is dismissed as of no value for practical devotion or for the application of Christianity to the affairs of human life. The doctrine must doubtless be regarded as a mystery; first in the New Testament sense of the word, since it depends upon revelation and could never have been attained by pure thought alone, apart from such a self-disclosure of God as the Incarnation entails; and secondly, it is a mystery in the sense that human thought can never wholly comprehend the Divine Essence, and therefore how God is both a Trinity and a Unity will always transcend complete understanding. But we shall endeavour to show that the doctrine is no alien importation into Christianity; if it is a growth, it is a natural and necessary growth if God is to be thought about in a way that shall remain true to Christ's thought of God and the New Testament thought of Christ; and so far from it being an intolerable burden to the intellect, it brings to it considerable relief. The abstract nature and the alleged aridity of the doctrine are only felt by those who have forgotten that God must be loved with the mind as well as with the

THE DOCTRINE OF THE TRINITY

heart, or by those who have unnaturally emphasised theological concern, while neglecting the devotion it is intended both to safeguard and call forth. In presenting Christianity to the modern world the doctrine of the Trinity does not need to be apologized for or kept in the background, but rather proclaimed as the solution demanded by thought, the sole sanction of our highest religious aspirations and the true inspiration of social life.

The doctrine of the Trinity, as finally formulated, is certainly the outcome of a gradual development, but it can be shown to be due neither to transformation nor to mere addition, but only to the necessity for a clearer explication of what is contained in the teaching of Jesus and implied in the faith of the New Testament. Its more explicit formulation was found necessary in order to shut out speculations which confused the facts of revelation and endangered the promise of redemption. We have previously seen that there can be no explanation of the appearance of Jesus Christ which does not trace this to the incarnation of a divine person, a person who is truly and eternally God. But if Jesus Christ is truly God, the question was bound to arise how this fact was to be reconciled with the truth, at all costs to be maintained, that there is only one God; for it will be admitted that, at least during His incarnate life, Jesus is personally distinct from His Father in heaven. If, therefore, Jesus is truly divine, it looks as if there are two Gods, and if the Holy Spirit is a distinct, divine personality, different both from the Father and from Jesus Christ, that there are three Gods. The New Testament prohibits this conclusion by constantly maintaining that there is only one God, and that God is one. But nowhere in so many words are we told how the divinity of Christ and the

THE DOCTRINE OF THE TRINITY

distinct personality of the Holy Spirit are to be reconciled with this fact; for the text which says, "there are three that bear record in heaven, the Father, the Word and the Holy Ghost: and these three are one," is not found in any but very late manuscripts. The solution proposed that Jesus is not divine and that the Holy Spirit is not a person is too crude and hasty to be worthy of consideration if the New Testament writings are to be taken seriously. We have previously shown that the first part of this solution is impossible, but it ought to be noted at this point that while the Arian solution would sink Christianity to the level of paganism, with its demi-gods, the Adoptionist theory, which would elevate Jesus to Godhead, or denominate Him as God in virtue of being perfect man, would involve either absorbing the personality of Jesus in God, or leaving Him indisputably a second God, and thus readmit polytheism. With regard to the second element in this solution, it need only be noted that while the divinity of the Holy Spirit is never denied, to make the Holy Spirit an impersonal influence, or simply Jesus Christ Himself in His present spiritual condition, does violence to the plain language of the New Testament, which speaks of the Holy Spirit in terms which have no meaning save in regard to a person, and sufficiently distinguishes the Spirit, both from God the Father and from Jesus Christ.

We need not examine the New Testament evidence in detail, for it will be admitted by all that, both in the Gospels and in the Epistles, there are constant references to three, and only three, personal realities in close connection, namely, the Father, the Son and the Holy Spirit. These three are constantly found bracketed together, and no others, persons or things, approximate to anything like the

THE DOCTRINE OF THE TRINITY

same relationship. Without going through all the references, it may be taken for granted that these Three are in some sense distinct, and yet are in some sense connected. This distinctness combined with connection is found most clearly expressed in the post-Resurrection saying of Jesus where He bids the disciples go and baptize all nations " in the name of the Father, and of the Son, and of the Holy Ghost." Here the three stand side by side, and yet are spoken of as but one name. The fact that this declaration is placed upon the lips of the Risen Christ, that according to the testimony of the Acts of the Apostles baptism was administered simply in the name of Jesus, and that the phrase is always quoted by one of the Fathers in an incomplete form, has been taken to combine sufficient evidence to make it impossible to believe that this statement should ever have proceeded directly from the lips of Jesus. This is, however, an unnecessary conclusion. The words do not prescribe the formula so much as the intention of baptism; the record in the Acts that believers were baptized " in the name of Jesus " also does not necessarily describe the formula used, while the Trinitarian formula is found very early. No manuscript exists without these words; they are natural to the occasion of their utterance, and the shortened quotation which is found only in Eusebius can probably be explained as an abbreviation. For as far back as the record of Christ's baptism we have a threefold manifestation, the Father speaking, calling Jesus His Beloved Son, and the Holy Spirit descending as a dove. In the Synoptic Gospels Jesus often speaks of the Father, of Himself as Son, and of the Holy Spirit, and although with definite marks of distinction, yet also in close connection. In the closing discourses of the Fourth Gospel, it is plainly

THE DOCTRINE OF THE TRINITY

taught that the Holy Spirit is distinct from Jesus and from the Father, that He proceeds from the Father, and is sent by the Son; and yet He is called "another Comforter," to take Christ's place when visibly removed, and it is promised that Father, Son and Spirit are to dwell together in the believer. We must put alongside these references the constant references in the Epistles to the same Three in similarly close connection. These need not be exhaustively detailed, but it can be pointed out that we not only get references where they stand side by side, as "the same Spirit . . . the same Lord . . . the same God," and especially in the well-known salutation, "The grace of our Lord Jesus Christ, and the love of God and the communion of the Holy Ghost"; but there is a necessary connection between all Three implied in such typical sayings as, "through Him (Christ) we . . . have our access in one Spirit unto the Father," and "praying in the Holy Spirit, keep yourselves in the love of God, looking for the coming of our Lord Jesus Christ"; and even the strange salutation from the Revelation: "from Him which is and which was and which is to come; and from the seven Spirits which are before His throne, and from Jesus Christ" (where "the seven Spirits" may be only a crude expression for the sevenfold Spirit), we get the same unique and unapproachable collocation. A similar usage continues in the Early Church in the doxologies, which bracket Father, Son and Holy Spirit together, so that it is much easier to think that the Trinitarian doctrine, at least in the form that Father, Son and Holy Spirit are each divine and yet that God is one, goes back to the earliest times and rests ultimately upon the teaching of Jesus. The more explicit formulation of the doctrine, and the reconciliation of the Trinity

THE DOCTRINE OF THE TRINITY

with the Unity of God, were necessitated through the rise of certain conceptions which were inadequate and unsatisfactory, and so at length a form was reached which both preserved the New Testament doctrine and attempted to answer the question how the three divine Persons were to be conceived as one God.

We must now examine some of the alternative and rejected solutions. The conception known as *Sabellianism* attempted to solve the problem by regarding the three Persons as nothing more than three aspects of God. But this is obviously excluded by the *personal* relationship of the Three, of which that existing between the Father and Jesus during His incarnate life gives the revealed, actual measure, while the description of the Holy Spirit making intercession for us compels us to assume His personal distinctness. What has been called an economic Trinity conceives of the Son and the Spirit as only put forth from the Being of God for a period, and then re-absorbed. This does not yield an essential Trinity, it imperils the permanence of Christ's personality and denies the unchangeableness of the divine nature. It is to be suspected that many people solve the problem of the Trinity by regarding the three Persons as three parts of God, who only by being added together make up the one God. But this denies the proper deity of each Person insisted on by the Athanasian Creed and involves the impossible idea of the partition of Deity. On the other hand, it is to be feared that many fall into Tritheism. But toleration of the idea that there are three gods is utterly abhorrent to the monotheistic character of Christianity and the constant affirmation of the New Testament that there is but one God, and is a betrayal of the early Christians who died rather

THE DOCTRINE OF THE TRINITY

than have anything to do with polytheism; while not only does the unity that Jesus claimed with the Father, both in essence and will, equally with the reiterations of the Athanasian Creed shut out Tritheism, but to admit that there are three gods would imperil the whole basis of the revelation of God in Christ; for we should have no assurance that the three were alike in character.

Greek theology had endeavoured to secure the unity of the Godhead by a method of interior subordination in which the Son was made less than the Father and the Spirit again less than the Son. The danger of this hierarchic arrangement was the introduction of a descending scale of beings, less and less divine, inserted in between the One Supreme God and the creation. Subordinationism was inclined to pass beyond the realm of the truly divine, thus readmitting all the errors of Gnosticism. There can be no degrees of divinity; and in order to maintain this and exclude further error an advance was made to the declaration that the three Persons are co-eternal and co-equal. If this seems to offend against Christ's explicit declaration that the Father was greater than Himself, this is explained as referring only to Christ's incarnate condition, but is sufficiently safeguarded by the acknowledgment that the Son owes His being to the Father, while the Spirit owes His being to them both; though in each case by an eternal movement, in the one case called " generation " and in the other called " procession." There was an older formula of the doxology: " Glory be to the Father through the Son in the Holy Spirit," which, although perfectly capable of an orthodox explanation, came to be abandoned because it was being used in an Arian sense, and the doxology that had existed alongside it, " Glory be to the

THE DOCTRINE OF THE TRINITY

Father and to the Son and to (or, with) the Holy Ghost," became the accepted formula, and remains the most familiar confession of equalitarian Trinitarianism.

It should be noted that the doctrine as formulated in the Athanasian Creed provides very little in the way of further explanation. In asserting that each Person is God, and that these are nevertheless not three Gods, but one, it simply repeats what the Scriptures already maintain. Its only attempt at explanation is contained in the phrase "neither confounding the Persons, nor dividing the Substance"; which means that Trinity is affirmed of the Persons and Unity of the Substance. What Person and Substance mean when applied to the Deity we may be unable to comprehend, but at least we must not so define them as to make either the distinction or the unity unreal, or the one subordinate to the other. For instance, we must not lower the conception of person beneath human personality; if there is a difference between the two it is that divine personality transcends, not falls beneath the distinction and reality of human personality. This is endangered when "persona" is lowered to its original meaning of a mask. We know one Person of the Trinity, namely Jesus Christ, and that His distinction from the Father was enough to enable Him to pray to Him. But on the other hand we must certainly not lower substance to mere "nature," so that we think of the three Persons as simply sharing the same nature, as three human persons would share human nature. The Persons of the Trinity are so united in nature as to be indivisible: no one Person can ever be separated from the other.

It has now to be considered whether the doctrine thus formulated remains incomprehensible and therefore unacceptable to the intellect. It may be admitted that the doctrine of the Trinity is only a deduction from the facts of revelation and that this deduction is necessarily expressed in human terms; it may also be admitted that no doctrine can adequately express the essence of Deity, and therefore that the furthest refinement of statement concerning the inner life of Deity to which the Trinitarian doctrine can lead will always fall short of completely satisfying either the intellect or devotion. This does not mean that it is inadequate for intellectual purposes or confusing to devotion, but we must do more than think about God, we must worship and love Him; and until we see God as He is, and are united to Him, we shall not know what it is that the doctrine of the Trinity actually implies. What we know of the interior life of Deity we know only so far as God has revealed Himself and our intellect can comprehend what that revelation entails. Such terms as person and substance cannot describe the reality of God, and even the names Father, Son and Holy Spirit must be understood only by analogy, for they are human terms. But while the reality of God must transcend such terms, and remain finally incomprehensible, this is altogether different from saying that other terms would do equally well, that they are inadequate as doctrine, or that a reduced affirmation either of the threefold character or unity of the Godhead could be admitted. Indeed, it is possible for the human intellect to advance from the formulated doctrine of the Trinity by a series of analogies to a deeper understanding. Some of these analogies must now be examined.

It has been pointed out that a comparison of other religions reveals certain tendencies making on the one hand towards the supremacy of one god, and on the other hand to a triad of supreme gods. But such

THE DOCTRINE OF THE TRINITY

a movement throws no light on the process by which the Persons of the Trinity were revealed or the Christian doctrine was formulated. More may be derived from certain hints and foreshadowings in the Old Testament, where sometimes the divine nature is referred to in the plural, and, in the later books, God's Wisdom, Word and Spirit undergo a process of partial personification. But these are no more than hints; the use of the plural may be explained as the plural of majesty, and the personifications are obviously only poetic. Nevertheless they somewhat prepare the way for the further revelation. It has also been argued that in man's own constitution we may find an image of the Trinity; for man is body, soul and spirit. But here again the three elements which constitute man are by no means on an equal level; and an absolutely tripartite psychology which would make spirit really distinct from soul is to be regarded with suspicion. Again, human love seems to reflect the Trinity in its ideal combination of father, mother and child. But here the distinction of personality is carried too far to be an adequate analogy; they are not always one in any sense, and never one as the Trinity is. Finally, the necessities of thought which always employ the three terms of subject, object and their relation have been instanced as showing forth a trinity and a unity; but here the distinction between terms of thought falls short of the distinction between the Persons of the Trinity. All such analogies are imperfect. This does not mean, however, that the doctrine of the Trinity is therefore completely inconceivable or an inadequate analogy of God. We should expect the being of God to be both more simple and more complex than the being of man; we should expect man and creation to carry some image of the Trinity, but in an imperfect form. And it is not impossible to move, by the help of

THE DOCTRINE OF THE TRINITY

these analogies, to a somewhat clearer conception of their transcendent reality in God. We recognize that where love exists between two human beings an extraordinary degree of unity may be attained, though it never leads to anything that we can call unity of substance; but while it does not demand the absorption or obliteration of personality, a great degree of unity in will and even in thought can be attained. We have only to push this analogy of love still further to conceive how it could be possible in the being of God for there to be sufficient distinctness of persons to enable love to exist between them, and yet, since love is the very essence of Godhead, how this makes possible such an insight into one another's mind that it constitutes but one mind in God; even if we must suppose there to be three centres of consciousness in God, each would have access to the whole Mind; or we might conceive of the one Mind having three forms of consciousness. We can conceive also how God, being Love, if there are three wills in Him, yet in their action they are absolutely one. So God is one Mind, and one Being. This the doctrine of the Trinity further seeks to secure by the idea of the complete indwelling of the one Person by the other; while appropriating to each Person a certain form of activity as His own, yet conceives no action as ever taken by one Person alone, but always by the co-operation of all; so that the one always acts not only with, but through and for the other. We may have no earthly analogy and no complete intellectual comprehension of the Trinity, but the more we think truly and the more we love, the more the Trinity is seen to transcend, but not to contradict, our thought and love; it may outsoar the intellect, but it neither confuses nor burdens it.

It remains now to set forth briefly the value of the doctrine of the Trinity to thought, to devotion

THE DOCTRINE OF THE TRINITY

and life. It must be remembered that any values we may find are dependent upon its being true; but we should expect a truth of this nature to carry with it the richest of values. It enables us to think of God as a living reality containing the fullest answer to all human needs. It is very doubtful if the thought of God can be made rational or an answer to humanity's needs apart from the doctrine of the Trinity. The conception of a solitary monad with nothing but Himself to contemplate and to love produces in our minds the impression of that very self-centredness from which it is the very purpose of redemption to rescue us. And yet, if we have to go outside the Godhead in order to find a completion to His thought or love, then we surrender the self-existence and the self-sufficiency of the Deity. The philosopher finds it necessary to posit in God a certain movement of thought in order to save the conception of God from the stagnation of mere self-contemplation. God's thoughts are higher than our own, and their transcendence is perhaps to be measured by the fact that with God thought and reality are the same thing, and so even for God to think of Himself must make the object of His thought something more real than such thought would ever be with us. So we are bound to hypostatize the object of His thought in some such conception as the *Logos*, and if the Logos is thus hypostatized, the thought of both seems to demand some third uniting reality. But we rise to greater clearness and certainty when we think of God not only as Thought which demands some differentiation, but as Love, and there it is inconceivable how love can come to any fulness unless it has another to love, while merely mutual love would be imperfect unless it was united in loving another. So we pass beyond the abstract

THE DOCTRINE OF THE TRINITY

necessity of hypostatized thought to a community of persons in which alone love reaches reality. Some form of Trinity seems demanded if God is a Mind, and there must be a clear distinction of persons in the Trinity if God is Love. The Trinitarian conception therefore saves the idea of the Godhead from fruitless self-absorption and stagnant inactivity without having to borrow anything from without in order to complete the conception. The interior life of the Godhead must be conceived as eternal pulsations of infinite love; first from Father to Son, and then from Father and Son uniting in the love of the Holy Ghost, thus constituting a perpetual movement of the highest life and the purest bliss. And if it is Love that needs the personal distinction, it is Love that secures the absolute unity. Therefore if the essence of God is love, then both the Trinity and the Unity seem to follow. The doctrine of the Trinity also gathers up all that was craved in polytheism, and yet reconciles it with absolute monotheism, without that inhumanity and aridity to which sheer monotheism with no distinctions within the Deity has often given rise.

The doctrine also holds great values for devotion. It enables different types of mind to approach God from different points, and yet to reach the heart and the whole; the philosopher's love for the transcendent and the scientist's interest in creation may bring them to God through the conception of the invisible Creator and eternal Father; the love for humanity and history may lead to God through the Incarnation of the Logos in the humanity of Jesus; the person concerned with interior experience and social fellowship may come to God through the communion of the Holy Ghost. And yet we can come into contact with no one of the Persons without coming into contact with God and with all; for

THE DOCTRINE OF THE TRINITY

each Person is God, and none is separated from the other; to know one is to know the others, for each is like the other in person and identical in substance. Moreover, the fact that distinction of persons is eternal in the Godhead, and not merely something temporary that has to be absorbed, shows that our own union with the Godhead does not entail destruction or absorption of our personality. It must be remembered that the end of our redemption is personal union with Christ, and that union carried to such a transcendent point that it involves nothing less than participation in the Godhead. In union with Christ, and in dependence upon Him, we are brought into that living movement of Love which constitutes the Godhead; for we become co-heirs with Christ, we share the glory which He had from the beginning, and the love which the Father has for the Son now becomes the love for us, for we are incorporated into " the Beloved." This is the real meaning of the so-called baptismal formula; it is not to baptize *in*, but *into* the Name of the Father and of the Son and of the Holy Ghost. It means that we are brought into the life of the Blessed Trinity, lifted up into that tremendous circle and movement of love. All this would be impossible if God were not a Trinity; for otherwise the union of a human personality with God would be the introduction of a new thing into Deity, demanding either that God Himself was incomplete, or that we should have to cease to be ourselves in becoming united with Him.

The doctrine further contains the most fruitful idea for application to actual life. Man cannot mirror God in loneliness, but only through union with his fellows; it therefore takes a society rather than an individual to image God. This explains why it is that a man must love his neighbour in order to love God; there can be no merely lonely

THE DOCTRINE OF THE TRINITY

love of God; we cannot confess God in isolation; we must love one another in order to be united to Him; and therefore part of the expression of our faith must be a society in which difference of personality and unity of basis must be equally maintained. Therefore the Trinity sets before us the ideal of a social order in which the human family shall bear some resemblance to the Godhead; neither allowing personality to develop into individualistic anarchy, nor personality to be swallowed up in an absolute state. So far from personality therefore being a mistake and a hindrance to unity, it must be maintained in order to make that unity real and rich, while personality depends for its completion on fellowship with other personalities. Hence redemption is perfected on earth in the fellowship of the Church, in heaven in the fellowship of the Trinity. In the Church the Holy Spirit incarnates Himself in a society which becomes the Body of Christ, in which Christ unites all men to one another in Himself, and thus brings humanity into the unity of the Godhead, which fulfils the plan of creation and consummates the purpose of redemption.

XII

THE DOCTRINE OF THE ATONEMENT

THE doctrine of the Atonement is in reality very simple; it consists of nothing more than the declaration that reconciliation has been wrought between God and man by the death of Jesus Christ. This is undoubtedly scriptural doctrine; it goes back to the teaching of Jesus that He came to "give His life a ransom for many," and especially to His declaration concerning the cup at the Last Supper: "This is My blood of the covenant which is shed for many unto remission of sins." The Fourth Gospel adds to this teaching the declaration that Jesus was "the Lamb of God which taketh away the sin of the world"; likens His death to the lifting up of the serpent in the wilderness, so that "whosoever believeth may in Him have eternal life"; and compares it to the act of the good shepherd "who layeth down his life for the sheep." These Gospel statements show that the value of Christ's death is in its being a defence of mankind against danger, sufficing to ransom them from captivity, effecting the remission of their sins, and healing those who look to it in faith. The Apostolic doctrine seems to do little more than reiterate and illustrate these ideas. St. John, in agreement with St. Paul, regards the death of Christ as a propitiation; the writer to the Hebrews regards it as the only sacrifice which can purge our sins; St. Paul emphasizes the purpose of Christ's death as a reconciliation

THE DOCTRINE OF THE ATONEMENT

and effecting our redemption, and teaches that the death of Christ enables God to justify those who have faith in His blood.

Now it must be evident to thoughtful readers that these statements are based upon the idea that there was something peculiarly necessary about the death of Christ, and about the actual form that it took in the violent shedding of His blood, if the forgiveness of God was to become effective in redeeming men from their sins; and that without such a sacrifice justification and reconciliation were impossible. But wherein this necessity consists, and how its efficacy operates, does not seem to be clearly stated. It would be easy to suspect that the efficacy of the old sacrifices provided the basis for the atoning value ascribed to Christ's death, but such efficacy is precisely what is repudiated. It is this apparent lack of explanation which has given rise to the various theories of the Atonement.

It must be remembered that these theories constitute no part of the doctrine of the Atonement; no one of them has been sanctioned by the Church as sufficient. Different theories have been put forward in succession, have gained temporary acceptance, and then, on being subjected to critical examination, have dropped out of favour. It is an interesting fact that while the Church has felt bound to decide what is the true theory of the Incarnation, no such decision has been felt necessary concerning the true theory of the Atonement. This is probably to be traced to a number of facts: firstly, that the Scriptures seem to assume or sanction different theories; secondly, that the contemplation of the Cross by faith is so effectual in producing an assurance of forgiveness and reconciliation that to those who have this assurance

THE DOCTRINE OF THE ATONEMENT

an explanation of its efficacy is not felt to be necessary; and thirdly, the necessity for a clear theory of the Atonement has only been deeply felt since the Reformation, and controversy on the subject has been almost confined to Protestant thought, concerning which a Catholic decision has therefore been neither called for nor sought. A further reason for the comparative unconcern of Catholic Theology might be suspected in the continual observance of the Eucharist and belief in the sacrificial character of the Mass; for it is possible that this perpetuation of the Sacrifice of Calvary and the mystical identification with the Passion by participation in the Body and Blood of Christ either sets forth a satisfactory theory or lessens the necessity for any theory. Protestant theories seem to owe their origin to the desire for an assurance of forgiveness which can be shown to have a legal sanction or be capable of logical proof; whereas Catholic instinct seems to be satisfied with the assurance set forth in the crucifix and the effect conveyed in the Communion; though this distinction is very general and cross-filiations could be pointed out on both sides. There can be little doubt, however, that the widespread diffusion, at least among Protestants, of a theory which is believed to be scriptural and orthodox has occasioned considerable revolt in the modern mind against the very idea of the necessity, the possibility, or the efficacy of the death of Christ as an atonement for sin. With the language of Scripture apparently resting on some ideas or theories, not however explicitly stated; with the modern repudiation of practically all extant theories as irrational, unintelligible or spiritually inadequate; and with the irrepressible desire of

THE DOCTRINE OF THE ATONEMENT

man to understand the mysteries of the Faith and find a clear basis for the assurance of salvation, it is vain to propose that we should be content merely with a preference for this or that theory, or to dispense with all theories whatsoever.

It will be most convenient to outline what has been widely considered, particularly amongst Protestants, as the orthodox theory of the Atonement. It can be summed up as follows : Christ's sufferings were the penalty due to sin, His blood was accepted as the equivalent of what man owed, and therefore was a substitute for man's condemnation and the propitiation of God's just vengeance, carrying forgiveness of all sin, and the imputation of Christ's righteousness to those who accept this plan of salvation. We need not investigate the sources or authority for these doctrines ; it would be found that few reputable theologians would support them in their entirety, and in this form ; and yet it cannot be denied that this theory has had a strong hold upon popular belief, can be found expressed particularly in hymns, and has been believed to rest on a scriptural basis. It is only with this last point that we need here concern ourselves. It is a fact beyond dispute that while the Scripture continually states that Christ died *for* us, this cannot be extended to mean that He died *instead* of us. Our English preposition " *for* " is ambiguous, but not so the Greek, which must be translated " on our behalf," rather than " in our stead." Further, it is not only said that Christ died for us, but that He rose again for us ; and no one would dream of suggesting that His resurrection was a substitute for our own. Moreover, the Christian is held to have died with Christ, and it is declared that it is only as we die with Him that

THE DOCTRINE OF THE ATONEMENT

we rise again with Him. Whatever being united with the death of Christ may mean, it is carried so far as to demand that we must be crucified with Him. According to Scripture, therefore, it is more true to say that Christ died that we might die with Him than to say that He died in our place. Again, it is perfectly true that the Scripture unmistakably declares that Christ's death is propitiatory; but the strange thing is that it never says who is propitiated; and it must not be assumed that this must so evidently be God that there is no need even to state it, for whenever reconciliation is spoken of it is never declared that it is God who has to be reconciled to us, but always we who have to be reconciled to God. The question of whether Christ's righteousness is *imputed* or *imparted* to us has been a source of great dispute between Catholics and Protestants. It might be thought there was scriptural basis for the doctrine of imputed righteousness, but this is denied by Catholic exegetes, and whether it is scriptural or not, belief in it has now been almost entirely surrendered by thoughtful Protestants. It will be seen that the popular theory at every point presses the language of Scripture beyond its own carefully observed limit or reticence. Yet this type of theory seems so necessary to complete and explain the language of Scripture, that it is not surprising that it has been taken to be scriptural; and, even when this is disproved, that suspicion should remain that this is the theory Scripture assumes, even though it may not be stated; and that the rejection of this theory must disown the doctrine of the Atonement altogether. This conclusion might find support in the fact that the word "atonement" has now disappeared from the Revised Version

THE DOCTRINE OF THE ATONEMENT

of the New Testament; and rightly, for the word had gathered to itself a meaning which it did not bear when it was used by the Authorised Version; for then it meant " to make at one," which was a correct translation of the original Greek, which simply means " reconciliation "; whereas the word " atone " has come to mean make reparation by some substitutionary act satisfactory to the person wronged. But it would be entirely superficial to give up the word " atonement " because of this changed use, and then to imagine that we had solved our problem. The very fact that the word has changed its meaning is an indication of man's idea that some atonement, in the later sense of the word, ought to be made. And even although the aim of Christ's death is " at-one-ment," reconciliation rather than reparation, the question still remains why His death should be necessary for that purpose.

This consideration of the meaning of the word " atonement " forms a natural transition to a task which must now be, however briefly, undertaken, namely, to inquire whether before the Reformation or outside the popular Protestant theory any more adequate conception of wherein the Atonement consists can be found. It is interesting to notice that the dominant idea among the Greek Fathers seemed to have been that the Atonement was effected by the Incarnation. It was the making of man and God one in Christ which was the at-one-ment. But this idea cannot ignore the fact that the death of Christ sealed that atonement, and if Christ had refused to drink this cup it would have torn asunder the divine and the human in Christ, and thus have dissolved the Incarnation. The Greek Fathers did not overlook this issue, but its critical importance

THE DOCTRINE OF THE ATONEMENT

was perhaps neither sufficiently recognized by them, nor is it in any conception of the Incarnation which does not regard the death of Christ as both the ultimate purpose and the necessary fulfilment of the Incarnation.

When, however, some of the Fathers came to consider why it was necessary for Christ to die, they fell back upon His own word about His death being a ransom; but when they went on to inquire what was the price of the ransom, and to whom it was paid, they came to the conclusion that Christ's blood was the price, and the Devil the person to whom it was paid. They regarded this ransom, however, as a kind of bait which the Devil grasped at, under the delusion that he could retain Christ, for which prize he was quite willing to release the human race. Although this idea held such mighty minds as those of Origen and Augustine, it has come to be regarded as unfair, almost profane, and bordering on the ridiculous.

It was our own St. Anselm who gave the death-blow to this theory and replaced it by the idea that Christ offered something to the Father which man owed but could not pay, namely, the satisfaction of divine justice. That demanded from us a life of perfect obedience, and since we have failed to yield that, we are in debt; and even if we could now pay our debt, since that would only be our due, it would offer no satisfaction for our original offence. St. Anselm believed that because Christ was divine, His death outweighed all that was owed by human sin, and so divine justice was satisfied. It is evident that this theory is open to serious objections; one will suffice. God could not possibly be satisfied with anything less than the complete obedience of man, and it is difficult to see how the

THE DOCTRINE OF THE ATONEMENT

death of Christ could be taken as in any way an equivalent for that, unless it can be shown to be the means of bringing about that obedience.

Abelard tried to supply the defect in Anselm's theory by insisting that it was God's love which dictated the death of Christ, and it was the display of Christ's love in that death which wins the heart to repentance and to God. What is lacking in Abelard's view is a clear conception of why the love of God should have chosen this particular method of display, because love, even at the cost of supreme sacrifice, does not awaken love unless there is some necessity for the sacrifice.

The Scholastic doctrine retains the notion of satisfaction, but makes the death of Christ not the only or absolutely necessary satisfaction, but a sacrifice which God's love moves Him both to accept and provide. This has continued in the main the Catholic doctrine.

It will probably be felt by many that the combination of the three ideas of love providing the sacrifice, the sacrifice making the satisfaction, and the completeness of the satisfaction being due to the infinite value of Christ's sacrifice, conceals rather than strengthens the weakness of each separate idea when taken alone. For if the sacrifices of the Old Testament are unable to take away sin, to say Christ's death is a sacrifice does not explain its efficacy. This sacrifice obviously surpasses all others in merit because of Him who made it, but it is difficult to see how this merit actually makes a satisfaction for human sin, save on some quite arbitrary principle. And while it is the love of God which prompts the sacrifice, and we thus get rid of any idea that Christ's sacrifice is to avert the Father's anger or win the forgiveness of God, there

THE DOCTRINE OF THE ATONEMENT

is no explanation of why this sacrifice should have been a satisfaction to His love. And if we recognize that it satisfies His love because it has the effect of winning men to Himself, this in turn involves the difficulty that it does not have this effect unless the necessity of the sacrifice is realized by men.

We shall not find that these remaining difficulties are much relieved if we turn to other theories which have been proposed since the Reformation. It was the theory of Grotius that God only demanded this particular kind of satisfaction for the purpose of satisfying governmental justice, that is, for the prevention of the lax ideas which would have arisen if sin had been forgiven without any one being punished. But this offers no solution, for the punishment of the innocent instead of the guilty would hardly help to maintain respect for the justice of God. It was Macleod Campbell's idea that what Christ offered was not so much vicarious suffering as vicarious penitence; but although this seems to come nearer to the truth, it fails to provide a complete theory, for it does not show why Christ's penitence should have taken this sacrificial form, or how His penitence could have been a satisfaction for ours.

The felt and admitted unsatisfactoriness of all these theories of atonement may be traceable to three causes: a lack of reference to the historical facts of the Crucifixion; the lack of contact between theories and the vital results which must flow from Christ's Cross and Passion; the inadequacy of any theory that can be compressed into a statement when compared with the rich content and vivid experience of the doctrine of the Atonement. The first of these causes we may be able to remedy; the second demands a vital process which a theory

THE DOCTRINE OF THE ATONEMENT

may describe but which only the Cross itself can effect; and the third may be achieved by an attempt to combine the various theories.

If the actual historical circumstances of the death of Christ, some setting forth of which has been previously attempted, were kept in mind, theologians would not have wasted so much time trying to discover why it was that Jesus had to die and to shed His blood in order to secure our salvation; for this had to be primarily because man compelled Him to this. It was a human rather than a divine necessity. In confirmation of this it is interesting to note that in the development of Catholic thought on the Atonement which succeeded Anselm's theory, Abelard, Thomas Aquinas, and Duns Scotus agree in repudiating the idea that the Atonement could only have been wrought by the particular method by which it was actually effected. They repudiate any absolute necessity for this, and fall back upon God's mercy, love and choice. But with this repudiation of strict necessity, there seems to remain a certain element of mere display and arbitrariness, unless recourse is made to the necessity forced upon Christ by human design and historical circumstances. An examination of these elements reveals that their fear, envy and hate were such that men could not tolerate the challenge and claims made by Christ and were not satisfied until they had subjected Him to every species of cruelty and insult in order to emphasize the completeness of their rejection, and, by the death and shame inflicted on Him, put an end to the Son of God and His appeals, so far as this earth and their own hearts were concerned. For man's sin in the Crucifixion mounted up to the height of attempted deicide. If men had believed Christ's claim to be

THE DOCTRINE OF THE ATONEMENT

the Son of God, they would have realized that it was impossible to destroy God; but they thought they could at least destroy His love, and it is this which makes their sin not only such an affront to the Divine Majesty, but even a sin against their own hope and the highest within themselves. But while it is true that there is no need to make such a mystery of why Christ had to die, and it is really unbecoming to man to propose as a problem of divine necessity what was entirely his own manufacture, nevertheless, it cannot be overlooked that in taking the line of the Incarnation, the inevitable conflict with man which led to the Crucifixion must have been foreseen; but the necessity which man's sin imposed upon God to undergo this humiliation and suffering was willingly accepted by His mercy and love; for it was the divine purpose to transform man's act of sin into the divine act of Redemption. This purpose was in order to reveal to man the measure of God's love, and how impossible it is for man to change it; also, in order to assure man of God's free forgiveness, by taking the worst sin that man could ever commit and by the bearing of that sin making it the proof and seal of the divine forgiveness. The Crucifixion could not frustrate the intention or change the love of Christ, and in the Crucifixion, therefore, man has the proof that there is no sin which God is not willing to forgive.

This reference to the actual historical facts of the Crucifixion and Christ's attitude in bearing the Cross seems to satisfy the statement of Scripture that His death was a propitiation and a sacrifice which takes away sin. In the death of Christ God provides a propitiation, neither of Himself nor of man, but, as the Scripture simply states, a propitiation for sin; that is, something which takes sin at its worst, and so changes its consequences that, instead of that sin becoming, as in the normal course violent bloodshed always does, the seed of fresh sin, it "speaketh better than that of Abel" whose blood cried for vengeance from the ground, and speaks only of God's forgiveness. This way of interpreting the Cross not only rests on the realism which the Creeds reiterate by appealing to the plain facts that "He was crucified, dead and buried," but it also seems to do justice to the conceptions involved in the theories which have gathered about the ideas of ransom and sacrifice. Our Lord does not state to whom His ransom was to be paid; it obviously did not need to be paid to God, and Christ could not recognize the Devil to have any right to hold humanity; yet behind the curious Patristic notion that the Devil was outwitted by the death of Christ, we can see a most valuable idea and one that is entirely true. The powers of this world, as perverted by the Devil, and the forces in which men, deceived by him, have come to put their trust, were turned against Christ in the hope that if only He could be condemned as a criminal, overwhelmed with shame, and proved impotent, His claims, His attraction and His power would be completely destroyed. By submitting to death Jesus allowed men to make trial of their powers, and He proved they were absolutely impotent. Men hung Him upon a gibbet of shame, and He made that cross the very symbol of hope and victory; they pierced His heart, but they could not kill His love; they shed His blood in the violence of their hate, and that blood became the most precious sign of the length to which His love would go for us. By this act our Lord destroyed

THE DOCTRINE OF THE ATONEMENT

the dominion of the Devil, for He proved his boasted power to be utterly impotent against His own naked, unarmed love; and so He ransomed men from the delusions in which the Devil had bound them. Again, while all down the ages man had been trying to make some sacrifice which he believed would satisfy God and bring the assurance of forgiveness, yet although those sacrifices entailed the cost of life and the price of blood, the idea had always been at work that it was " impossible that the blood of bulls and goats should take away sins," and that this was not what God actually desired. These sacrifices had probably arisen only as an attempt at reparation for sin and as a substitute for man's failure truly to offer himself, and so were after all only a substitute and inadequate, accepted by God under the old dispensation, because they were all that man could offer to express his sorrow and contrition, and because they were training men to understand the sacrifice of Christ. But the superiority of Christ's sacrifice is: first, that it is provided by God Himself; secondly, that it is the sacrifice of the Sinless One; and thirdly, the essence of it is Christ's uttermost offering of Himself to the Father in order that He might bring about the remission of man's sins. But in interpreting the Atonement as secured by sacrifice, we must be very careful that we do not interpret Christ's sacrifice by the Levitical ritual, but rather the other way round. For there is no efficacy in the mere shedding of Christ's blood as such; the essence of Christ's sacrifice was the giving up of His own will in obedience to His Father for the love of man; the blood is merely the sign of how costly that sacrifice was, and therefore how far His love was willing to go. The sacrifice of Christ does not secure the forgiveness of God; it was God's willingness to forgive that provided it. The shedding of Christ's blood does not change the attitude of God towards us, but it does give man an absolute assurance of God's forgiveness; for in the sacrifice of the Cross and in the shedding of the precious blood man sees the sign and seal of that forgiveness.

But all this would remain still very imperfect, and would not give us a complete theory of atonement, unless we could show how the remission of sins is secured and redemption is actually effected. Now it is a fact that there is nothing like the Cross of Christ for inducing both repentance and faith. When man sees that all his sin issues eventually in an act like the Crucifixion, if anything will bring him to repentance, it will be this. He sees the suffering it has caused the Innocent One, he sees that God endured this for love of him. This vision of what the Cross means does not generate saving power except by faith; but faith, here as elsewhere, has its roots in a natural and rational attitude towards facts. Man's natural attitude towards the Crucifixion is abhorrence of the deed and pity for the sufferer; and when he is willing to consider the facts which caused the Crucifixion, he is bound to realize his implicit responsibility for Christ's death; for this is what all sin in intention actually involves. It is then that he is ready to cry for that gift of illuminating faith which enables him to see that his own sins were there borne by Christ, and that he himself was included in His universal forgiveness. If that faith is a true, living faith, the faith that works by love, the Crucifixion of Christ has a double effect upon the heart of man. It crucifies " the world ": it puts an end to all its attractions, temptations and bribes, for man sees that it was "the world" that crucified Christ. It also crucifies self; for it makes it quite impossible to live any longer to oneself when this is seen to be what corrupts human personality, and perverts the world from the purpose for which God created it. Christ's display of His love for us wins for Him the central place in our hearts, and thus there begins to take place a close knitting to Christ through the Cross. His personal friendship is there offered to us, and we begin to share His mind; He begets in us the acceptance of His life laid down for us, and He begins to pour that same life through us. The blood of Christ, that is, His life laid down at such a price, cleanses us from sin by bringing the assurance of forgiveness; blots out the guilt of sin by the way in which He bears its sorrow on His heart and removes the effects of its stain from our minds; and brings about the remission of sins by destroying our very love for sin, and taking away any further taste for it. And now the redeemed soul of man moves on to a process which can only be called identification with Christ crucified. He accepts the offering of Christ for himself, but makes it in spirit and in intention his own offering; and through constant communion with the Crucified the spirit of the Cross becomes his own. The blood of Christ is not only shed for him in love, changes his taste and his values, but it becomes by a mystical transfusion the very life-blood of his own soul, seeking to pour itself out in service, and, if needs be, leading to a laying down of his life in turn for his brethren. The identification is so real that not only is the soul sanctified in union with the one offering of Christ, but henceforth man so lives by the spirit and intention of the Cross that he bears about in his body the dying of the Lord Jesus and lives what is virtually a martyred and crucified life.

Now it is this effect which makes it possible to apply the word " satisfaction " to the sacrifice of Christ, and relieves the term of that appearance of mere legality, substituted payment, and calculating equivalence which has often come to be associated with it and has imparted to it the notes of unreality and hardness which have secured its wide repudiation. If we only remember what it would be that would " satisfy " the heart of God, we shall see that God would not be satisfied merely with the punishment of anybody, the sinner or Christ ; for the effect of sin means the death of the soul. God willeth " not the death of a sinner, but that he should rather turn from his sin and be saved " ; and anything that would effect that would be a satisfaction to God. In so far as the Cross makes a perfect provision for all men to be assured of their forgiveness, whatever their sin, if only they care to accept the offered mercy and respond to the call of Love, this satisfies the heart of God, because it secures the fulfilment of His purpose which sin had frustrated, by leading men to repentance and faith.

And since, finally, the Cross secures to those who are willing to see its truth, understand its meaning, and accept its conditions, that filling up of the sufferings of Christ which man can make by living a life of reparation and sacrifice, and so attaining at last, by the help of grace, to the vision of God and union with the Divine nature. It is this which Christ secures that constitutes the merit of His sacrifice, that is, the divine perfection and power of it, on which man is able to draw for

THE DOCTRINE OF THE ATONEMENT

inspiration, and by which he is able to live after the same fashion.

It now simply remains to be shown that this closer linking up of the theories of the Atonement, both with the historic facts of the Crucifixion, and with the saving effects of the Cross, satisfies, first of all, the Catholic development of the doctrine of the Atonement. For it rescues the old theories from anything that seemed, as in the " ransom " theory, a deceptive device, in the " satisfaction " theory a stretching of the law of justice, or in the " display of love " theory a mere theatrical manifestation; it retains the idea that the form of the Atonement was a human rather than a divine necessity; and it satisfies the instinct that man, fired by the example of his Redeemer, must offer his own penitence and sacrifice, doing this by the communion which the Sacrifice of the Mass mystically effects, and reaching out towards that identification with Christ crucified which alone will take him along the mystic path to final union with God. At the same time it does gather up what Protestant theories have sought to secure, without involving those conceptions which have at length brought such wholesale revulsion. Protestant theories have always been jealous to secure that man's salvation owed its origin and power entirely to God. This is not, however, infringed by the demand that Christ crucified for us is ineffectual until He is crucified in us and we are crucified with Him. But this necessity, whilst guarding against the unethical substitutionism and tendency to antinomianism which the popular Protestant theory has always been in danger of inducing, does nothing to derogate from the fact that it is the perfection of Christ's sacrifice and

THE DOCTRINE OF THE ATONEMENT

His actual work in us which makes any sacrifice on our part acceptable or possible. It is still not something we do which constitutes and wins our atonement, but something Christ did for us on the Cross. But all that is not simply an act buried in past history; it is the revelation in time of the eternal love of God. So the sacrifice of Christ is in essence an eternal thing, and it must be wrought within us here and now if it is to be effectual. But this appropriation no more infringes upon the sacrifice offered once for all, than does the daily sacrifice of the Mass infringe upon the perfect sacrifice of Calvary; it is in both cases simply the same sacrifice; for that which is wrought in us is not our doing, but Christ's work within us. This interpretation also embraces what is valuable in the Protestant theory of Christ's vicarious penitence; for it enables us to see the sense in which He bore our sins. He bore not only the consequences of our sins, in the hatred which planned the physical sufferings of the Cross, but in His pure conscience He felt the burden of the sin we ought to have felt; it was in that sense that He took our sins upon Himself and bore them up to the Tree. While the mob were mocking and His murderers were doing their worst, He felt with such bitterness, as only the Sinless One could feel, the utter hatefulness, and horror, and stain of sin. In His profound love for men He felt their sin as if it were His own, and in this sense He became "sin for us who knew no sin." He imparts to us His own conscience to waken us to a sense of sin and to penitence for it. His penitence is only vicarious in the first instance; He feels the sin in order that we may feel it, not in order that we need not.

THE DOCTRINE OF THE ATONEMENT

Finally, this penetration of the theories with historic reference and effective results enables us to return to the language of devotion with an unhesitating and undistracted mind. The daring and vivid metaphors which are embodied in the liturgies, the prayers and the hymns of the Christian Church, can be accepted wholeheartedly, because their inner meaning is now revealed, their metaphors are not pressed beyond their intention, and they are relieved from all possibility of misunderstanding. Even the doctrine of substitution, which has been so difficult to many, can be accepted with the limitations that are now placed upon it. We can still sing " in my place condemned He stood "; for the condemnation that the world hurled upon Christ was really the condemnation which our sins ought to have brought upon ourselves. We do not go on to say we must never bear that condemnation; that is precisely what we shall have to do: bear the condemnation of an accusing conscience; for the Cross of Christ was caused by our sin, and it is our condemnation. But at the same time it is the proof that there is no more condemnation for those of us who have been crucified with Christ. So we can still sing

" Let the water and the blood,
From Thy riven side which flowed,
Be of sin the double cure,
Cleanse me from its guilt and power."

The guilt of our sin has been the attempted murder of God, but the Crucified One has risen again for our justification; He has shown that He cannot be murdered, that, despite all, His love has remained unchanged, unhurt; moreover, the self that crucified Christ has died with Him, and has thus paid its penalty and passed away; and so our guilt is doubly done away. The power of sin over us is broken by the disclosure of what sin means, and the attraction of love for Him who bore it. It enables us to take up again the vivid metaphor of the Precious Blood and to feel its cleansing power, to see into the innermost meaning of the Mass, to drink that cup which becomes in us His most noble blood, the love that pulses in our heart and courses through our veins. We can return to our simple devotions before the crucifix, knowing that here is all our hope, for here is His abundant mercy, and here our sufficient assurance; here is God's satisfaction and ours, the perfect offering which God Himself made for our sakes. It shall be our satisfaction too when at last we shall wake in His likeness to praise Him for our redemption, and become one with that love which planned the Incarnation, accepted the Crucifixion it involved, made that Crucifixion the turning-point and the seal of our reconciliation with God, and so loosed us from our sins, and made them as though they had never been, washed white in the blood of the Lamb.

For Product Safety Concerns and Information please contact our EU representative GPSR@taylorandfrancis.com
Taylor & Francis Verlag GmbH, Kaufingerstraße 24, 80331 München, Germany

www.ingramcontent.com/pod-product-compliance
Lightning Source LLC
Chambersburg PA
CBHW050635300426
44112CB00012B/1806